TIME

ISN'T THE PROBLEM,

YOU ARE

TIME ISN'T THE PROBLEM YOU ARE

Four Strategies to Transform STRESS *Into* SUCCESS

CHAD E. COOPER

New York

TIME **ISN'T THE PROBLEM,** YOU ARE

Four Strategies to Transform STRESS *Into* SUCCESS

Published in New York, New York, by Morgan James Publishing. Morgan James and The Entrepreneurial Publisher are trademarks of Morgan James, LLC.
www.MorganJamesPublishing.com

We are committed to both the quality of our products and the service we provide to our customers. We value your comments, please feel free to contact us.

Factive Nautics Coaching
CoachCooper@ChadECooper.com

For more products and information, visit our website:
www.ChadECooper.com

Use this QR Code to validate your book purchase and get access to additional valuable content only available when you use this code. Thank you for your purchase and support!

ISBN 978-1-63047-700-4 paperback
ISBN 978-1-63047-701-1 eBook
Library of Congress Control Number:
2015911258

Cover Design by:
Rachel Lopez
www.r2cdesign.com

Interior Design by:
Bonnie Bushman
The Whole Caboodle Graphic Design

To my son who I trust will make his life fulfilled through the clarity of knowing what he desires, courage to go after what he wants, gratitude for receiving it, and persistence to see it through.

To my wife who is the love of my life and strengthens me.

TABLE OF CONTENTS

ACKNOWLEDGEMENTS

To everyone who helped me make this dream a reality and for believing I could reach even one person, but plan to impact multitudes. A special thank you to:

Janet Cooper — For helping take the words in my head and turning it into something others can understand!

Marc VonMusser — For countless support, patience, and encouragement. For the spark that started this whole journey; my friend. Your heart is awesome!

Mom — For always being my cheerleader and believing in me.

Kelly Sullivan Walden — For ensuring the spirit was present and fun along the way.

Dana Walden — For keeping true to your insights and keeping it real, respectful, helpful, and impactful.

Debbie Weisman — Without whom this book would not have come together; Miracle worker.

Steve Wasko — My longest friend and dream supporter along so many journeys together.

Chuck Vallie — Being an example that change can happen whenever we decide.

Patty Cooper — For showing what creative can be.

Dale Cooper — The example of steadfast conviction to live to a higher standard and being himself.

Jayne Jewell & Brenda Schinke — For helping to hold me to my own standards and doing it in love.

Dan Michalek — Reminding me that All is possible through God.

INTRODUCTION

"And in the end, it's not the years in your life that count. It's the life in your years."

—Abraham Lincoln

You know that feeling. Maybe for you it happened when you opened your alumni magazine and read about your old roommate's latest achievement. Perhaps it came when you saw your neighbor pull into his driveway with a brand new luxury car. Or maybe it was the phone call from your brother bragging about the new diamond necklace he bought for his wife. I'm talking about that strange unsettling emotion, a combination of happiness for their success mixed in with some degree of envy, along with that multi-million-dollar question: *Why them?*

I'm betting that you've picked up this book because that question has been lingering in your mind for quite some time. Why do some people seem to work less and still receive a greater share of the pie? How are they able to navigate through the immense amount of information overload and live a satisfying, balanced life, while you stay up at night stressing out over how you're going to pay for that new roof? Why are they on item 128 of their dream list, while you can barely get past item one?

Why indeed? That doesn't seem fair now, does it?

Every day we're bombarded with news about people around the world who are living extraordinary lives, from the Silicon Valley executive showing off his latest yacht to the adventurer climbing the five highest mountains in the world. The media would like to have you believe they are exceptional, lucky, and somehow smarter and better bred than you.

That's a bunch of hogwash.

People such as Bill Gates, Sir Richard Branson, George Clooney, and Oprah Winfrey have led extraordinary lives, to be sure, but there's nothing in their DNA that makes them exceptional human beings. Yes, they are all talented. However, it was not their talent alone that brought them their success. There are scores of equally talented people who never reach their levels of achievement, and it's not for lack of trying.

What's their secret? There are lots of factors that go into their success. Study any of them and you will find that the most important factor has been their mastery of one very important part of their lives—something that made all of their achievements possible. This something is common to all people, whether you're male, female, rich, poor, educated, street smart, tall, short and everything in between. I call this the great equalizer.

One hundred and sixty-eight hours.

One hundred and sixty-eight hours is the number of hours in one week. I don't care how much money you have; you can't buy 169 hours. Week in, week out, there are 168 hours, and once you use them they're gone forever. Yet if they're used wisely, anything's possible.

People who live lives that matter know how to use their 168 hours each week most effectively. They are able to do this by being very clear in their purpose and passionate about what they do. They set goals and act on them consistently.

If you can do this, great. You're living your intentions, getting things done, and—unfortunately for me—probably don't need this book. However, if you can't do this, then yes, you've got a problem. A big problem.

All is not lost though. Wherever there's a big problem, there's also a big solution.

How can you—with the same amount of hours per week—replicate and produce the results that you want? How can you go from a life of working your tail off to a life of financial stability, freedom, and the happiness that comes from living life on your terms? How can you reignite your relationship with your significant other into something extraordinary?

Right now all of that might seem impossible, especially if you feel so overwhelmed with what life has handed you that you don't believe you have time for more personal development. In one sense that's true. You still only have those same 168 hours to work with. However, in these pages I will show you how to leverage those hours so that, with a few tweaks to your daily regimen, you can create a life that matters.

- More time to travel and vacation? Done!
- More quality time with a spouse or loved one? Done!
- More time to pursue hobbies or personal development? Done!

However...

(You knew there had to be a catch here, right?)

If it were just a matter of managing those 168 hours, there would be no real need for this book. If you don't believe me, type in the words "time management" into the search bar on Amazon.com. You'll come up with over 126,000 books dealing with the subject and over 5,000 books with the words "time" or "management" in their titles. That's a lot of writing and a lot of advice on how to effectively use your time to your benefit. Most of it is valuable. I'm such a big proponent of time management that I devote the last section of this book to my formula for how to make the most of those precious hours in your weekly life. It's important and valuable information, yes, but time management alone doesn't address the most important factor in transforming stress into success.

That key is YOU.

Yeah, I know. That stings. You want to believe it's something else—your boss, your co-worker, your spouse, your kid, the government, or the weather—that's keeping you from really getting what you want out of life. You want to believe you're giving your all. You want to believe there's another, easier solution than having to confront your weaknesses.

Here's something to consider. Go to the gym and take a look at that guy with those rock hard abs. He didn't get them from waving a magic wand over himself. He worked at building those muscles, something that took him time and effort. Success in life works the same way. Success just doesn't happen. The amount of success you achieve is directly proportional to the amount of effort you put into knowing yourself and how to use that knowledge effectively.

Let's get back to those reactions you may have had on seeing the achievements of others: That twinge of envy, that shock of surprise, or even outright bewilderment at how others succeeded where you haven't been able to up to this point. You may not have realized you harbor these not-so-nice feelings, and you may even be feeling a little ashamed, embarrassed, or upset that you do.

But before you throw this book across the room and give up in despair, take heart. You've done your best up to this point. You have the best of intentions and are frustrated by your inability to make things better and more productive for yourself. You just don't know how to transform your stress into success.

That's what this book is for. Consider this your how-to manual on how to make the rest of your life the best years of your life. This book is my way of offering you proven strategies that I've learned and tested so that you don't have to make the same mistakes I did.

I will teach you that you have the ability to be your own solution. I will show you the "how", to enable you to see that you are extraordinary and your dreams can become real again and again. But more importantly, I will also show you the "why", the impact that effects little changes in your routine will have on you, your loved ones, and your community.

HAVING A LIFE THAT MATTERS

In my time on the planet, I've had the incredible opportunity to be one of Tony Robbins' top tier Platinum and Master Coaches. I've taken my family on trips all over the United States, Caribbean, Central America, and Europe. Not only did I do the *Ironman* race, but I was sponsored by nine major companies, one which gave me a $13,000 bike, and I got to tour across the nation as a result.

More importantly, I've been able to be of service by being a leader to others. I've had the extraordinary privilege of serving on thirteen different charitable boards, and been an elected official for our city of 8,000 people. I've also had the honor of being named *Regimental Marine of the Year.* I've led missionary trips outside the United States, and brought children from the Chernobyl nuclear fallout zone into our home to help deplete the radiation from their bodies and bring nutrition and color back to their skin.

Most recently, I've led twenty other extraordinary people across the Grand Canyon and back in two days (46 miles) to raise awareness and funds for cancer and traumatic injury survivors.

I don't say this to impress you, but to press upon you that what I'm about to share with you works! These methods work every time and for everyone who applies them.

I've gotten to this point because I took the advice I give my own clients and told myself to be open to all possibilities and see how I could make them my own. I didn't let limitations get in the way just because other people said there were limitations. Ultimately, I came to see that my life is driven by one important rule: to put more into the world than I take out. That's what drives me when I wake up in the morning.

Even though I can say that my life today is extraordinary, I wasn't always surrounded by sunshine and rainbows. I'm not special. I wasn't born into privilege. I'm the product of divorce. My intellect is average. Sometimes my wife accuses me of doing some really dumb things.

That's the point. I'm no different from anyone else. I'm no different from you. I truly believe that anyone is capable of achieving what I have, if they too, have passion and the right tools.

While I say you're the problem, that doesn't mean that I think you're dumb. In fact, I believe you're smart. In fact, after working with hundreds and thousands of people, I know we all have significantly more power, and ability then we are using. After all, you took the time to buy this book, and I want to make sure you'll come to see it as the wisest decision you've made this year. You have everything you need to transform stress into success, right here in your hands.

LIFE DOESN'T HAVE TO BE HARD

When I was a young kid, I did a lot of things that held me back. Sometimes, when things didn't go the way I wanted, I felt like a train wreck. If I had not changed course, I would have been in the same boat as a lot of people—living a life of survival, instead of a life of unlimited possibilities.

I kept making mistakes that prevented me from achieving anything great. But I didn't question anything, because in many ways I was fairly comfortable. I had a job, a car, a place to live, friends, and a loving family. I was certainly in okay shape, especially compared to a lot of people, and for a long time that was fine for me.

However, when life is so-so or even okay, the tendency is to believe life will always be that way. The idea of becoming extraordinary was way, way off my radar.

In many ways, I was really just limping along. Like a lot of people, I limited myself to simple thoughts. My vocabulary for expressing emotions? Happy, sad, angry or pissed off. There was a lot of black and white and not much shading in between.

I had no grand scheme for my life. I wasn't really doing any planning. I was living a life of reaction. I was in a situation where I was working ninety hours a week and saw no way out. I was in an unhappy marriage, and for a long time saw no way out of that either. My life was all about getting through the day, paying the bills, having some fun on the weekend, and that was that.

I didn't have a purpose. I was just trying to survive. Trying to *thrive* wasn't even an option.

In short, I was subscribing to society's indoctrinated beliefs. Life is hard. Work for survival. If there's anything left over after the bills are paid, great, but don't necessarily count on any great rewards.

One day I woke up and realized that time was ticking by. I heard a voice inside me say, "It's time to live!" Then a moment later, the voice added a phrase, "But how?"

I embarked on a decades-long journey predicated on my desire for growth and to "be better". I began the process by tiptoeing outside my comfort zone and getting educated. I studied writings from Carl Jung,

Viktor Frankl, Napoleon Hill, Warren Buffet, Gary Chapman, Eckhart Tolle, Billy Graham, and David Deida. My education also included workshops and training with some of the masters in their fields: coaching giant Tony Robbins, financial guru Al Granum, and marketing genius Mike Koenigs, among others. I didn't go into any of those workshops feeling like "this one will fix me or fulfill me", but I trusted they would be a piece to the puzzle. That's why, along this journey I also engaged in much meditation and self-reflection work, trusting that the path I was on would bear fruit.

Like following breadcrumbs through a forest, I went from one inspired role model to the next, which eventually led me to discover my own system for success. I've taken pieces of these mentors' wisdom, and the insights I've gained in my years of coaching, to develop a strategy that, with commitment, practice, and persistence, can help you achieve everything you desire.

The system is based on my belief that there are four components of a totally fulfilled life.

- Time management
- Purpose
- Effective self-expression
- Operating from your highest self

It's also based on the premise that you hold the key to your own success. By truly understanding yourself and how to break free of the limits you impose on yourself, you can transform your life and the quality of your experiences, and create a life that truly matters.

I can't make the promise that getting all this will be easy. But I can promise that if you follow my suggestions you will have fun. In fact, I can wholeheartedly promise that if you come with me on this journey, you will find it absolutely worthwhile.

At the heart of doing this successfully is to have you create a winning life. Winning isn't a "sometime" thing, it's an "all the time" thing…and winning is a habit.

To have a winning life, I suggest you look in the mirror and say:

- *"I don't care about what other people say…"*
- *"I am more than what other people say I am."*
- *"It's time to live a life that matters to ME!"*

THE KEY TO GETTING RESULTS THAT MATTER

When I finally discovered my purpose, I started down the life path I'm on today. For instance, because I believed in the importance of giving back to my community, I followed in my grandfather's footsteps and ran for City Council of our small town. Since I've always wanted to mentor others, I've spent the past four years doing just that, with students at the University of Michigan. Discovering my purpose gave me the courage to live the life I love.

Being a father was important to me too. I desperately wanted to be a big influence in my son's life, but I came to the conclusion that being a great father was incompatible with my corporate job that kept me out of the house all day. I didn't want strangers to be his main caregivers. To be the type of father that I wanted to be, I realized I needed to be his major male role model, which meant being around for him. To do that, I had to retire.

I did. At the ripe old age of thirty-five, I retired from the corporate world and the ninety-hour workweek.

Guess what? Not only did I get the time to be a quality parent for my child, I got the opportunity to do lots of other fun things, like take annual trips around the country and learn new hobbies.

Some of you reading this might stop here and think that it's easy for me to say all this, because I have the time and the money to make these things happen, while you're sitting there wondering if you'll ever take another vacation again. Stick with me, please. Be patient. I didn't get here overnight. It took work, and a lot of planning and discipline—and I'll show you how you can do the same.

HOW TO GET THE MOST FROM THIS BOOK

> *"Are you an extra in someone else's movie script, or are you the lead author of your own blockbuster?"*
>
> **—Chad Cooper**

Do you want to learn how to live a life that matters? I know that you recognize you need to learn new tools, new methods, and to unlearn old unproductive habits that aren't doing you any good. Why else would you pick up a book that says right on the cover that you're the problem?

You're smart enough to know you have limitations and smart enough to want to do something to change them. There's a lot of ground to cover here, and throughout this book I'm going to ask you to look within yourself for answers by asking you questions you may never before have considered. I believe you have the answers within you, and I'm going to help you discover how to find them.

I'll be spending a large part of this book emphasizing the role that language plays in our lives. Here's a preview. Take the word *because.* When you think *because,* think *be at cause.* Don't get into the mindset of "I can't do this because" of this thing or that thing. In other words, be the *cause*, not the effect, of everything that happens in your life. You take a stand to make it happen.

Most of us will follow and live in the effect—that is, accepting what we get. That may be an okay way to live if you're happy settling for the crumbs of whatever may fall your way. But the likelihood is that you've picked up this book because that isn't what you want out of life. You want the whole loaf, right? In a life that matters—a life that's free of stress—you're somebody who is the cause of the matter, not someone for whom life just happens. When you settle for other people's actions or material things (these being "effects") you end up on the short end of the rope wondering how you believed it would lead to fulfillment, but it doesn't. However, when you are the cause, you shift the meaning and focus and your actions support your values.

How do you get started? One baby step at a time. To illustrate this, let's take the metaphor of the elephant. If somebody asked you to eat an elephant, you might look at the entire animal and go, "Why would I even bother? How could I ever begin to start?" The enormity of this beast might overwhelm you and make you want to give up right away. But if you concentrate on one little part, the whole doesn't seem very intimidating. Start with one item, one goal, one action, and move from there. Create a methodology and stick with it. In time, you will look up and realize you've devoured the whole thing.

Next, be easy on yourself. I don't believe in perfection. I don't believe that you should feel like you have to give up if you make missteps along the way. Think of it this way. If people come to a movie theater to watch the story of your life, what would they see? Are you an extra in someone else's movie script, or are you the lead author of your own blockbuster? Would they see an epic blockbuster or a bomb? If your life script was playing up on a screen, would people be bored or would they be mesmerized, saying, "I want that too"?

You'll notice also, that I'll be asking you a lot of questions. Take the time to answer them. Really? Yes, really. Sure, it would be easy for me to spout off the wise suggestions for self-improvement you'll see here and leave it at that. But those nuggets of wisdom would be forgotten the day after you read them, without the reinforcement that comes from your spending the time to figure out how they relate to your life and your goals. It's my way of saying you need to have skin in your own game.

It's never too late to start living the life of your dreams. One thing that helps is to surround yourself with people who will encourage you. Immerse yourself among people you want to emulate. That will give you the ability and the encouragement to continue taking more bites out of that elephant.

But please remember this. We're not talking about reinventing the wheel here. I don't want you to feel as if I'm beating you over the head with a giant re-do list that's asking you to recreate your life from the ground up.

That's not what this is. This is about making tweaks to the way you're already functioning, the way you're already operating, and changing your language and sense of purpose over time. Eventually your actions will morph into habits. When that happens, you're going to impact and influence your family. You're going to influence your boss, your friends. You're going to influence your community in the ways you're involved. But mostly you're going to affect and influence the relationship you have with yourself.

That sounds pretty good, doesn't it?

Are you ready to take this out for a test drive? Read on to discover how to move beyond survival, beyond stability, and into a life that has meaning and purpose.

One more thing before you really get started; studies show repeatedly that if you just read something you will only retain between 3% - 9% of the knowledge. However, when you write down your answers to the questions below and throughout this book, your retention goes up to 45% - 58%. Even more powerful, is once you write down the answers and implement them in action; you will reach 80% - 90%! I want you to get more than your time and money's worth, please take the time to write out your answers for each question in the book in ONE location, and then take action to become the solution and make your dreams reality

TIME ISN'T THE PROBLEM TAKEAWAYS:

1. Here's a list of at least ten things I want to do or accomplish.
2. In lieu of writing out the entire movie script for my future life (because that would be ridiculous), here is my next scene… including setting, sounds, and feelings.
3. The Universe just told me I have one month left to live. I am okay with living it just like I am now? Not really, so I am changing these two things.
4. I am exceptionally good and passionate about these things that I do right now.

STRATEGY ONE

LANGUAGE MATTERS

YOU ARE WHAT YOU SAY

"Your beliefs become your thoughts, your thoughts become your words, your words become your actions, your actions become your habit, your habits become your values, and your values become your destiny."

—Mohandas Gandhi

Lots of people like to quote Gandhi. Why not? He was a great man, who by his actions and integrity changed the course of an entire country. Who wouldn't want to listen to what he has to say?

That's the problem. People read this quote and tell themselves how sensible it sounds...and then do nothing about it.

Let's take another look at the message of that quote. Change your thoughts and change the world. Easy enough to say, right? Sounds simple enough. But how do you change your thoughts?

Do you simply tell your brain, "Stop thinking *that* and think *this* instead?"

In the simplest sense, the answer to that question is yes. But most people don't get beyond paying lip service to that thought, because change is hard. Some people would say it's impossible.

That's because that fuzzy stuff in our brain makes it hard for us to change. We keep managing to find reasons not to start or to give up before we begin. We come up with excuses—and we're all experts in creating every excuse imaginable—all in an effort to stay where we are. That place may make us feel miserable, but because it's familiar, we're content to stay there, rather than venture into the unknown world of change.

That's why, even if you tell yourself you need to change, you stay where you are.

I say, "Enough of that!" Life is too short to stay in a life of misery.

You might say, "Yes, Chad, you're right but where do I begin?"

If you are, in fact, truly ready to start on the road from stress to success, congratulations! Welcome to the journey.

Step one starts with language. Yes, language. Why? Simple. Language is the tool we humans use to communicate, and effective communication not only gets your point across to others but also to yourself.

You may be saying to yourself, "Come on, Chad. I write great memos. I speak clearly and distinctly." That may well be true, but is your language as effective as it can be? I bet not. We're all imperfect, and we all have a lot to learn. To prove this point, let's take a trip to one place where the English language resides: the dictionary.

According to the Oxford English dictionary, there are about a quarter of a million words in the English language. About fifty thousand of them are words that we don't use anymore – thy, thou, shalt, those kinds of words. Approximately ten thousand are emotional words, words that depict our feelings in the most descriptive ways.

Guess what? The average person uses about twelve of those words. Yes, *twelve words* to emphasize or elaborate their emotions.

Believe me, I was as guilty of this lack of self-expression as anyone. It reminds me of a *Saturday Night Live* skit where they mocked George H. W. Bush where he said, "There are two kinds of words: inside words and outside words. The trick is not to let the inside words get outside."

That's the problem, we behave in "appropriate" neutral and boring ways through dull language. My years of active duty Marine service had instilled in me a need to communicate my feelings in terse, simple ways. I was happy; I was sad; I was angry; or frustrated. That was about the extent of my dynamic language expression for a very long time.

Such black and white thinking doesn't translate well in the everyday world, where life is experienced in many shades of gray. I am not ashamed to admit that it took me a while, but I learned eventually that my language really influenced how I looked at and experienced the world. Expanding my vocabulary resulted in my becoming more fluid and allowed me to be more precise.

Let me give you an example. I have a family member who's a graphic artist. One day he showed me something he was working on, and I commented on how much I liked the blue color he was using.

"That's not blue," he pointed out to me. "That's slate."

"What are you talking about? That's blue," I insisted. I have eyes. I can see. I learned my colors when I was a kid. I know there are blue, yellow, red, and green. That's all there is. He said, "No. That's not blue. That's slate." He then took out a color chart and pointed to various shades of what I had, up to that point, simply called blue. "That's navy blue. That's royal blue. That's baby blue. That's periwinkle."

What he helped me realize that day is that language is very much like colors, with an infinite amount of shades. This is especially important when it comes to our emotional language.

Let's take the emotion of happiness. You can be happy but you can also have shades of happiness that really pinpoint what you want to experience. I can explain in terms of this book. When I set out to create this project, I asked myself, "What is the experience I want to have?" Happiness was right up there. I didn't want to put the time and effort into doing the work involved if I thought I'd end up upset or stressed. I wanted the project to be fun for me to do.

But there was shading to that. I enjoyed gathering together the information contained here. There was pleasure seeing the pieces come together during the editing process. A feeling of satisfaction came over me when I reread the manuscript and imagined the positive effect on others. That feeling mushroomed into elation the first time I held the finished book in my hands.

Therefore, the language we use, the actual words we use to communicate, can have a major effect not only on how we convey our intentions but also—and perhaps even more importantly—how we feel about our intentions.

The most common place I see language influence myself is when I speak. However, equally critical is the language I see people write on calendars and to do lists. More on this to come, but just be aware of where your language is subtly influencing you right now.

BEWARE OF LIMP LANGUAGE

Now, let's put language awareness into practice as we take those first baby steps down the road of transforming stress to success. I believe strongly that in order to craft achievement in your life, you need to put your plans into action, and that one way of keeping you on track is to keep a detailed schedule of your daily activities. (In the next chapter, I'll discuss this in greater detail.)

The words that you use to notate these activities have an immensely powerful effect on how you feel about them. Language matters. If one of the lines on your appointment schedule says *workout*, what does that mean? An hour to celebrate your body and how healthy you are? Or an hour of drudgery in an effort to stay in shape? Do you see the difference in the emotional impact of both of those meanings? You're the one who makes this determination. Which is it? There's no way of knowing, if the only word in your vocabulary is "workout".

A word like "workout" is an example of what I call *limp language.* I use the word *limp* specifically to give you a visual association. Think of limp bacon or a limp dishrag, and you get the idea. Limp is not a word you want to hang around your neck. Acting limp is not flattering and neither is talking in a limp manner. Limp language is flat and has zero energy.

Sadly, we're all guilty of using limp language without realizing its impact upon us. However, if we took the time to truly think about what we're saying or putting down on paper, we might make different choices.

Take an expression that most of us have used often at one point or another: *I have to drop off the kids.* Look at those words, especially the first three: *I have to.* Do you really believe that dealing with your kids is like a prison sentence, something you're being forced to do against your will?

Of course not. You love your kids. (At least for the purpose of this exercise we'll make that assumption.) Therefore, wouldn't a more celebratory way of expressing the same situation be more along the lines of "I get to drop off the kids"?

A lot of times we fall into limp language because there are other things going on in the background. We might feel upset or guilty about leaving our kids to go to our jobs or whatever other activity is keeping us away from them. Since we're not spending that time with them, we describe the activity of dropping them off in a negative way. Somehow it's supposed to ease that guilt, though most likely it doesn't.

But before you go hanging your head in shame or lamenting all those years you've spoken in this manner, take heart. All is not lost. Just a few simple tweaks in how you speak or write down your intentions can make a powerful difference.

Here's how I describe the process of *dropping off the kids*. Twice a week I carpool for my son and his friends, but I don't say *dropping my son off at school*. Instead I tell myself, "I have safely traveled, spending quality one-on-one time transporting my son to school." That is literally the subject line I enter on my appointment schedule. The phrase completely explains both the action and the emotional intention I *really* want to experience.

I started getting into the habit of doing this back when I was still in the corporate world. Needless to say, this practice raised a few eyebrows among my colleagues. I got reactions like, "Have you gone off your rocker? It's not socially acceptable to put that kind of stuff in there. What is wrong with you?"

Sometimes that's what happens when you propose a new idea. The naysayers come out and want to knock you down, almost like a reflex, without any consideration of the merits of the thought.

The ironic thing though, is that within two weeks they came back to me, every single one of them, and said, "That crazy little idea of yours really stuck in my head. It's weird, but tell me more about it."

Getting into the habit of being this deliberate with your language takes practice. Admittedly, using this terminology can also be a bit awkward and clunky until it becomes so second nature that it's an organic part of your life. Frankly, I can't think of a better way to be aware of your language consistently than in your schedule because it's in front of you daily!

Now, let's dive deeper into why I made these deliberate word choices in my schedule.

Language changes how the world looks. In the subject line I'm very specific about asking, "What is the experience I want to create?" I don't *have* to drop off my son. I *get* to drop him off. It's something I want to do; therefore, it's how I want to describe it. The phrase, I *have safely traveled,* means that I travel or leave with enough time to deal with construction, congestion, or an accident. I also make sure there's nothing going on that might make me feel anxious or stressed out. This includes quality decisions about my driving behavior, which means everything from remembering to signal all lane changes, to refraining from flashing certain hand gestures at people who might cut me off when they forget to use their turn signals!

Quality one-on-one time means that I'm not on the phone with somebody else when I have the opportunity to talk with my son. I'm not listening to the radio while he's on a tablet or smart phone, and we're in the same physical location but totally disconnected.

By expressing this desire for quality time on my schedule, I'm actively declaring that this is the experience I want to have. This makes my intention much clearer than the slightly negative notation of *dropping my kids off.*

DEFINITIONS COUNT

Another important aspect of language is the way we define words. One word that has a lot of meaning for me is *divorce.* My parents were divorced, and I can't tell you how many people looked at me when I was growing up with that pained expression on their faces when they uttered the words, "Oh, you're a victim of divorce."

Even back then, way before I'd developed this whole philosophy about language, I knew there was something very disempowering about that phrase. I never felt like a victim, and all the negative connotations that go along with that, just because my parents were divorced.

Believe it or not, I saw the divorce as a blessing. In my opinion, I was better off than kids whose parents were together. Since both of my parents got remarried, I would say to naysayers, "I get to choose the best qualities from four parents. I could pluck what I love from each of them and leave out the stuff I didn't like."

This was a different way of looking at the situation, a different way of using the language—a deliberate choice on how I wanted to see things.

Step one on the evolutionary growth path is to take greater care in the words you use to describe your daily tasks. Take a major step on this new path by creating a habit of using affirming words in your subject line and putting aside the default words that—without you even realizing it—have been holding you back all this time.

TIME ISN'T THE PROBLEM TAKEAWAYS:

1. What does my schedule look like from yesterday? Wait, I didn't write down my schedule yesterday, so this is a list of everything I did. Isn't it interesting how I describe my actions?
2. This is my schedule for tomorrow; and if I do not have it documented, here is a list of things I want to get done tomorrow. I can use this new method of description, based on the experiences I want to create, and make a new juicy and delicious schedule or list that looks like this. (It's weird seeing a Marine write the words juicy and delicious, but we are all so much more than our titles).

PITFALLS OF THE TO-DO LIST

"Life is what happens to you while you're busy making other plans"
—John Lennon

Ah, the to-do list. Everyone wants to believe that if they have a to-do list and they just get everything done, then they'll be complete.

Unfortunately, it rarely works out that way. Why? Because the list can never be finished! Let's face it; there will always be more to do. Have you ever completed every single item on your to-do list? Yeah, I didn't think so. I know that as soon as I get something done, I'm already thinking about ten more things that need be added to my schedule.

There will always be more to do than time to do things. To-Do lists create mental clutter. It's time to declutter your environment. Mark Divine says, *"When your clutter isn't bogging you down, you literally and metaphorically have more room for the things you need."* Therefore, the goal is to prioritize, but most likely you don't know how to do that effectively. Most likely, your to-do list feels like a giant boulder you're pushing up a mountainside with a Q-Tip. You feel it's insurmountable, and your natural response is, "Why even bother?" (Remember that elephant from earlier?)

What do you do? You take the easy way out. You steer away from the hard choices and look to do the things that feel comfortable or feel good right now. You'll even create a great story, justification or defense about why it's really important not to tackle the to-do list. As a result, you procrastinate.

That is, until you're left with no other choice. "This is really urgent!" you tell yourself, with the appropriate level of panic in your voice. But it's urgent only because this item previously was a to-do that you procrastinated on. What's so seductive (notice language choice) is that it's true, kind of.

Or you might take a different approach. Maybe you're the type who lives by the philosophy of, "let's see how life unfolds today". If you create a to-do list, you ignore it. More likely than not, you have no planned agenda for the day. Or if you do, perhaps the list consists of random, separate "Post It®" notes scattered across the room.

What's the result? You'll get whatever happens, including the good, the bad, and the indifferent. Instead of you controlling your life, you end up letting life control you. Remember the living in effect versus be at cause? Compare your schedule to perhaps Bill Gates, Oprah, Dwayne Dyer or others you may admire. You may say "I don't want their lives" and I get that, my question is if you believe they are doing well in life, is their calendar clarity richer than yours? If you don't want to be as busy, and Lord knows most of us don't, you'll just have bigger blocks of time for events then them perhaps. You see people who get great experiences daily have clarity in how their day will unfold.

I'm betting you want more out of life than chance. What might happen if you rephrase the question and ask instead, "What do I want to experience today?" You might discover that by asking this question and following through on your schedule, you will get exactly what you want.

- *What do I want to experience today?*
- *What am I willing to give in return for experiencing the day this way?*

WRITE IT DOWN! YOUR SCHEDULE IS YOUR BEST FRIEND

Here's what most people will do. They'll keep stuff in their heads or tell themselves that they'll get things done. What they're doing is setting themselves up for failure. They have ideas for what they want to do, but they don't allow enough time for completion. Even though they know there's twenty-four hours in a day, without realizing it, they've planned twenty-eight hours' worth of things to do. They end up feeling stressed out, frustrated, and incomplete. Why? Well, our brains play things out in our head kinda like a movie trailer. We get a bunch of great scene clips that look really compelling, but then when we go to execute them they take far longer than anticipated.

The result? You feel conflicted. You aren't enjoying yourself. You see others getting the things they want in life and that stresses you out even more.

Your life doesn't have to be that way.

Now, I know what you're thinking. You've gone through life carrying your agenda in your head and have managed to do so without forgetting anything. What's to be gained from writing it down?

Well, a funny thing happens when items get transferred from the head to a calendar. Action happens. Things get done. Plans are enacted. Progress is made.

Then there are those things you never think of writing down; your dreams, those big plans you hope to achieve someday, even items on your bucket list. Setting these things on paper has the effect of making them real, or at least potentially achievable, and suddenly they take on new meaning.

Now, let's get down to the mechanics. I use scheduling software that seamlessly connects to all my electronic devices. Many people, however, still use the traditional pen and paper based calendar or planner. While I find the older method a bit more limiting, either will work.

The key element is the language you use. The use of words that convey the energy of the appointment can be applied to either an online or paper document.

This vocabulary is especially critical in the subject line. When you look at your day on your calendar, is it enhanced by the language you use to describe its parts? If your words are limiting, if you're using limp language, then you're going to be constrained.

Ask yourself the following question: If this activity is scored on a scale of 0 – 10, with 10 being incredibly joyful, how would you rate the language you use to describe it? Unless you are scoring a 7.5 or higher, you need a rewrite. Again, look for the phrasing that's going to make a powerful statement about the intent of the appointment. If your software or planner is short on space in the subject line, use that space for a few powerful words representing the beginning of that appointment. Then add an asterisk or some symbol that says, "Hey, I need to look at the body of this appointment for more information."

There's a reason why a phone, desktop, or an online calendar has the space for the details of an appointment. Use that space and make reference to it. This space is where you can really spell out your empowering intentions. For example, if you have an appointment with your internist, on the subject line you can write, "*11:30 healthy chat with Dr. X*". In the body, you can expand that to say, "*Semi-annual assurance that my body is running at peak perfection by getting recommended tests and procedures*".

Again, this concept may sound clunky and awkward. But give it time. Repeat this practice over and over until it becomes a habit. By continually making the effort to add emotional meaning to your schedule, eventually you'll notice a change come over you. Feelings that were once remote, such as excitement, anticipation, and determination, will now become second nature.

HOW TO TRANSFORM LIMP LANGUAGE

OLD WAY	NEW WAY
Staff Meeting With Boss	Connecting for big commission time Aligning agendas to serve others Influencing mgmt. to support raving fans Influencing mgr. to position for promotion Gaining clarity & listening time Playing the same music sheet time Because = Be@ Cause Time Aligning agendas and futures time Partnering to mutual successful futures
Raking The Leaves	Play time with family in a pile of leaves Charitable time cleaning up others' yards Fun exercise in the great outdoors Tidy Up Time
Helping Kids With Homework	Quality 1: 1 time Planting mustard seeds Changing the family legacy Catapulting kids future success

Fixing A Leaky Faucet	Prepping the house for massive market profit Beautifying my wife's environment Plugging Holes Time!
Getting Teeth Cleaned	Prepping to a hot date w/ my honey Lowering my overall long-term bills Ensuring I enjoy a juicy steak time
Paying Monthly Bills	Ensuring Retirement ahead of schedule Working towards financial freedom while respecting and honoring my spouse

DEFINING YOUR ROLES

The next important step is to sort all of your activities. Most calendaring software has a feature called categories. But instead of considering everything in your life broken down into categories, a more empowering method is to re-label categories by calling them roles you want to experience in life.

What do I mean by a role? This takes a little bit of self-examination. You play many roles in your life. Some parts are ongoing, including your roles of spouse, parent, employee, and a boss. Sometimes you're a scheduled participant, such as your role as a gym-goer, grocery shopper, dental patient, bank depositor, and bill payer. Underneath certain roles may be subcategories or sub-roles. Under career, for example, you might have your role as employee and a role as boss in a side business for yourself.

- *Make a quick simple list of your Roles. To help many have a role as Career, Money/Finance, Health, Friends & Family/Relationships, Spouse/Significant other, Personal Growth, Fun & Recreation/ Personal Time, Physical/Health, and don't forget Celebration and Contribution (The last two we forget too often)*

COLOR YOUR WORLD

Once you have made a list of your roles, assign a color to each of them. The purpose of this is to make each appointment stand out in the schedule you will be creating. Generally, I find five to seven or eight colors are more than sufficient for you to color code your appointments.

The colors serve another purpose. They represent emotion. Each color gets assigned to the experience that you want to have, so the task doesn't become a *to-do*. It becomes an I *want to*. The color frames the meaning.

As an example, as I've learned to see more colors as an evolving man, the role of spouse is represented for me as the color purple.

I'm not going to tell you what color to assign to a role. While "purple for spouse" works for me, you might resonate more with the color yellow. You might want to assign green to all financial related roles and orange to health. Or not. If this is to work, you need to feel comfortable and make this your own.

The other great thing about color coding is that it gives you an easy visual of how much time you spend on any role in a given day or week. That way it's easier to gauge if you're devoting too little or too much time to the role.

Regardless of how you keep your schedule, whether on a computer, smartphone, or paper, there is an easy solution for color coding. Most calendars on computers have colors built into the program. If you are a pencil and paper kind of person, guess what? They make pencils in color! It really won't take up much room and you'll be impressed with the results. Give it a try! Visually oriented people will LOVE this tip because you will be able to quickly comprehend what your day's experiences have in store for you just at a glance. "Oh, I need to get ready because orange color means I have to be somewhere", as an example. Or, "Fantastic, I have only green the remainder of the day so I can relax and unwind!"

Often I find that when I become stressed, I can look over my calendar and quickly see I am excluding certain colors from my week. This usually means I'm out of balance. If I don't have enough green, for example, that means I'm not taking enough personal time to recharge. Duh, no wonder why I'm getting stressed!

TIME ISN'T YOUR PROBLEM TAKEAWAYS:

1. Here's a list of five roles in my life.
2. These are the colors that I have assigned to each of these roles. I chose these specific colors for these specific reasons.
3. Eliminate, outsource, leverage, and delegate commitments, obligations, beliefs, and even relationships that no longer suit me so that I can focus on what's most important.

THESE SILLY PHRASES MAKE A BIG DIFFERENCE

"Live so that when people think of adventure, excitement, and quality values they think of you."

—Chad Cooper

When I first started to use my languaging system, I wanted a term to describe my wife. Sure, I could have simply used her name, but I was looking for a word or expression that would convey the feelings I have for her and a name just doesn't do that. I never liked the word *Spouse* all that much either. For me, the term lacked energy and passion—a perfect example of limp language. This bothered me because I love my wife, and I certainly have plenty of passion for her.

I needed a more descriptive term. At first, I started using *Atlas Spouse*. You know who Atlas is…it's the Greek god who holds up the world. I saw my role towards my wife as the strong and powerful man Atlas, lifting the weight of life off her back to allow her to be more radiant. By this definition that term seemed appropriate.

But the problem was that over time, *Atlas Spouse* got heavy and arduous. I got mixed up with the image of holding the weight of the world on my shoulders, and our marriage was starting to feel heavy, exactly the opposite of what I wanted. That's not how I wanted to see her.

Worse than that, the term also brought out feelings of resentment and of being a martyr. That image of me holding the weight of the world morphed into, "Look at all I'm doing to take the weight off you in order to make your life easy." I didn't want that either. This was a lesson on why it's important to choose carefully the language you use.

Spouse was passionless. Atlas Spouse was toxic. I needed new terminology. My evolution brought me to the new term *Radiance Worshipper*.

How did I get there? My role in being a spouse is to bring out and worship the radiance in my wife. Therefore, when I schedule things to do with and for her, I am already pre-programmed with positive feelings about what I intend to do.

Here's a breakdown of how using this term shows up in practice. One of the ways that I can experience and create radiance for my wife is by doing something that most people consider a chore: cleaning house. "Cleaning" or "Beautifying My Wife's World" is now an opportunity to serve and honor her. What do I get in return? Her radiance. It's that easy.

I should add here that by describing this task in such a positive way, I also transformed my feelings about cleaning.

I'd learned how to clean when I was in the Marine Corps, by surviving what was called the white glove treatment. Literally, the officers would put on white dress uniform gloves and run their fingers over your work to make sure you hadn't left any dust or dirt residue anywhere. By passing The Marine white glove test, trust me, I earned a doctorate in cleaning.

The only thing The Marines didn't teach me was how to love to clean. Because I wasn't thrilled or excited about cleaning, I'd be thinking, "This is boring, this is not fun, this is heavy. I should be outside blowing stuff up. (I was a combat engineer.)"

I know I'm not alone in this. That's how many of us look at cleaning.

I should correct myself here. This is how I *used* to look at cleaning. I changed my attitude by asking myself that question, "What is the experience I want to have in this?" The answer was that I wanted my wife to feel pleased about being in a clean house. This was something that was very important to her.

This is now expressed in my schedule. In the subject line, I write, *clean house – beautifying my wife's environment.*

As a man, when I perform this role, I feel like I've climbed Mount Everest. When I serve my wife that way and see her radiance come out, I win. I feel great. I feel significant. I feel certain that I'm making her feel happy. I can connect that love with her. I've contributed to her. But again, that's the language. I don't *have to* do this task: I *get* to do it to her standards and be able to have her say, "that's what I was looking for."

Again, what's most important is to use language that honors where you want to be. *Spouse* may have a very positive meaning for you, and if that's the case by all means use it.

- *What's one item where I can transform the language in my relationship with that someone special?*

LANGUAGE IS AN ADVENTURE

By the way, my role of father is *Superdad.*

In my role as *Superdad*, I'm involved through action in my son's life. *Superdad* is the guy who uses the carpool ride for quality bonding time.

Superdad is also the man who finds a way to honor his son's desires while still taking care of his own needs. *Superdad* is not the guy sitting on the couch watching the football game drinking a beer. I do that occasionally, but I don't make that my habit. I'm not playing *Superdad* when I'm doing that.

For example, I brought my son on a business trip, and one morning when we were sitting in the hotel room he announced, "Dad, let's go to the swimming pool."

Now, as a busy man I'm thinking, "I've got a lot to do today. I don't know if there's time." Also, I looked outside, and sensed a chill in the air. My first impulse was to say no.

Then I took a step back and looked at the language I was using in my head. What was I telling myself? *It's going to take time. It looks too cold.* These were heavy and difficult thoughts. Even more pointedly, they were all about *me*.

I stopped and asked myself, "What do I *really* want this day to be like? What's the experience I want to have?" The answer was that I wanted to have an adventure with my son. That's the reason I'd brought him with me on the trip in the first place.

"Yes, let's go to the pool," I told my son.

As soon as I made the commitment, I knew I'd made the right decision. Once I told myself I was creating an adventure, I was inspired to do something I might not otherwise have done. It would have been a lot easier to say, "I don't want to do this. It's inconvenient."

But as *Superdad*, I had an agenda—to create memorable experiences for my son. I honored my son's request by using language that inspired me to say, "Why not? Let's just go swimming."

Now mind you, this really did end up being an adventure. We weren't talking about bright sunshine and ninety-degree weather. The hotel pool was under a cloud cover in a fifty-degree Southern California winter. We donned our suits, saw our breath in the air, and took a cold plunge into the water for a swim we'll both remember for the rest of our lives.

- *If you have a role as a parent or special someone, how can you transform your language and role into something that generates the experiences you want to make?*

HOW TO MAKE CHORES FUN

Here's another example of how I use language to illustrate one of the roles in my life. I don't like the terms health or fitness, so I came up with the role of Green Lantern when I take on those roles. Why Green Lantern? Simple. As a kid, he was my favorite superhero.

Green Lantern was this pretty buff human, who turned into a magnificent, physically chiseled superhero. Equally important to his physical strength was his mental fortitude. Green Lantern was picked to be a superhero because of his character and the values he represented. He didn't misuse his power. He honored and maintained his values and had rules that supported them.

Okay, let's see if you get my point here. How do you think I show up whenever I see a calendar appointment marked as Green Lantern?

Hint. I think about how I can physically hold myself, and how I can apply Green Lantern's superpower traits to my own needs. I think about his beliefs and how important they are to me. I embody all those ideas. When I go into that role I'm able to perform it with precision, enjoyment, and pleasure.

- *How am I showing up in my role of physical health? What role can I now give it that is really powerful, feels good, and is good for me?*

I don't take on this role only when I'm exercising. I also play the role when I'm executing a task such as mowing the lawn. One of the reasons

I mow my yard is because I look at that time as "me" time. The whole process takes about an hour—I have a relatively large yard and use a tractor—and it's such a pleasurable experience that I feel as if the world fades away and dissolves.

Sound funny? Most people look at mowing the yard as a chore. Not me. I look at this task as my time for abundance. Yeah, abundance. I consider this as my time to let the world melt away in a beautiful place I love, while being responsible and productive. I also get to multitask. Mowing the yard is a workout and keeps me physically fit. At the same time, I'm also entertaining myself by listening to music or an audiobook on headphones, or I'm being productive by listening to educational materials.

- *What is the name for my role in personal time?*

HAVING IT ALL

Most of the time we can't multitask effectively. But those times when you can fit several roles into one activity can be very special. Once, I was able to live five roles just in doing one experience, one activity, and that was when I led that trip into the Grand Canyon I mentioned in the introduction.

How did that happen? I had always wanted to take my family to the Grand Canyon. One Sunday I scheduled an hour on my calendar to plan how to turn that wish into a reality. During that time of thought, I remembered I'd had the opportunity to establish a friendship with an extraordinary woman, Robyn Benincasa, who is a three-time Guinness World Book record holder and the most winning adventure racer in history. She runs a charitable organization that leads people across the Grand Canyon. I contacted her and I asked her how I could support her cause, and that led me to doing a fundraiser at the Grand Canyon with twenty other coaches. My family also got to join me.

On that trip I got to fulfill five important roles: *Abundance*, *Radiance Worshipper*, *Green Lantern*, *Missionary*, my term for being a service leader and contributor to others, and *Bodhisattva*, my term for a wise, sage which I take on in my role as a coach.

ROLE PLAYING

ROLE	JUICY DESCRIPTIVE LANGUAGE	EMOTIONAL COLOR
Spouse	Radiance Worshipper	LAVENDER
Father	Superdad	RED
Physical Health	Green Lantern	GREEN
Service Leader	Missionary	BLUE
Personal Time	Abundance	YELLOW
Travel	Excursionist	ORANGE

I choose to refer to my personal time as *Abundance*. Personal time is extra time where I can do what I please, but the phrase "personal time" is a textbook example of limp language. The words hold no emotion or intent. But the word *Abundance* is different. When I hear that word I feel gratitude and appreciation for everything I have.

I've also learned to create abundance, not for it to just fall in my lap. When I look at my schedule, I make sure I have enough. To make *Abundance* stand out for me, I've given this role the color green, because green happens to be my favorite color. Green represents a lot of positive qualities to me. If I look at my calendar and don't see a lot of green there, I tell myself, "You know what? I'm not creating enough abundance in my life. What effect is that having on me for the day or for the week?" The additional benefit is that many people feel they don't get enough personal time, but in *Abundance* I feel gratitude for the time.

Another example is travel, which I define as travel to the grocery store, to get gas, or across the country for some exotic vacation. My role for travel is *Excursionist*. This role encourages me to be the adventurer. I can be an *Excursionist* while doing what some would consider mundane tasks, such as taking my son to a play date, sporting event, or to school.

I can even be an *Excursionist* in bumper-to-bumper traffic. I can choose to be the explorer who looks for and finds really intriguing or interesting things, rather than the guy who grumbles, "This sucks. I'm stuck in this traffic." As an *Excursionist,* I'm open and curious to whatever may be in front of me.

Contrast that with someone doing the same kinds of tasks who shows up in the limp language roles of *errand runner* or *taxi driver*. How do you think those roles would play out on the movie screen they're watching?

For most taxi drivers I know—and I can think of a New York taxi driver as an example— their pictures wouldn't be all that flattering. A taxi driver wouldn't think twice about showing up in sweat pants and a torn T-shirt. They're a slave to their kids. They feel like they're indentured servants forced to drive them around. It's a "have to" not a "get to" situation for them.

Meaning is everything.

If you're playing the role of taxi driver, I invite you to think of a more empowering metaphor that would serve the outcome and the experience that you are looking for. Use something that's exciting, something that turns this chore into serving and connecting, and something that contains variety. Have fun with it.

I have many clients who are faced with the turmoil, agony, responsibilities and all the heaviness of taking care of elderly parents. For them, I offer up the suggestion of a superhero character or somebody else whom they admire. Mother Teresa is a great example of that. She helped the poor and those who couldn't help themselves.

If you're in this situation, casting yourself in the role of *Mother Teresa* or some other empowering figure (my mother uses the role of

Sunshine Giver) can transform your idea of this work from *heavy lifting* into something more empowering like *joyous service*.

As I told you, I'm an elected official in my community. I chose *Sir Thomas More*, the patron of politicians, as my model and label for this role. I'm not Catholic and that doesn't matter. In this case, the term is useful to me and that's what counts. When I take on this role, I show up as a willing and joyful servant to my constituents. Everyone wins.

TIME ISN'T THE PROBLEM TAKEAWAYS:

1. This is one thing I have to do that I consider a chore. I can start calling it this to make it a want to do instead of a have to do.
2. This is the role I have assigned to the special someone in my life (special someone could be spouse, child, parent, B.F.F., etc.). This language is going to improve my connection with them, and here's how.
3. Retitle the subject line on an appointment that reflects this new title and make it a "get to" event.
4. I possess these qualities that give rise to or support an "I want to do this" opportunity.

GET WIRED FOR SUCCESS

In these last two chapters I've shown you how I use language to transform how I react to and act in the various roles in my life by using specific creative descriptive words. Now you may have bristled when I suggested you do the same, thinking you have to be a great wordsmith or walking thesaurus to do so.

Uh-uh. Not so. Anyone can develop their own personal empowering vocabulary. All it takes is understanding your VAK.

Your WHAT?

VAK.

No, it's not short for vacuum or the name of some alien. VAK is an acronym for how to craft your language powerfully and effectively. It consists of three elements:

1. Visual
2. Auditory
3. Kinesthetic

We are wired to look at the world in these ways. Each of us is more attuned to one than the other. If you find yourself stuck for the right words to use to describe roles and tasks in your schedule, look at the VAK for inspiration.

If you're a visual person, the language you're going to use is. "Do you see that? What does that look like?" If you're auditory, you're going to say, "What does it sound like?" If you're doing something, you might describe it as *the symphony.* It's an orchestra. You're using auditory language to represent how you represent the world. If you're a kinesthetic person, you're going to say, "How does that feel? Tell me if you were to touch that." "That's Hot!"

Ask yourself how these three ways of being resonate with you. When you create your schedule, the more that you can project your personal VAK into the subject line, the more that you can put that into the body, the easier for you to change your experiences from a "I have to" to "I get to do this."

Let's go back to the example of my cleaning the house for my wife. On my schedule I write down *Beautifying Surroundings as Radiance Worshipper*. I'm a visually dominant person, so the choice of color is important to me. I highlight that action in my schedule in purple because purple is the color I associate with my wife and it reminds me it's an activity I'm doing for her. The words *Beautifying Surroundings* tell me this is something pleasurable to do that will also bring pleasure to my wife.

The auditory in this instance would be the language I use to describe the action, something like VRRMM to indicate the sound of the vacuum. The kinesthetic, the touch and the feel, is conveyed by asking the question, "How does that feel for me?" That feeling is conveyed in the words *Radiance Worshipper* and the color purple. More accurately, the color to me is lavender. I can smell the lavender which is delightful. I can see a lavender field which is clean and pretty. Both of which I

JOE'S SCHEDULE FOR SUCCESS

	SUNDAY	MONDAY	TUESDAY	WEDNESDAY	THURSDAY	FRIDAY	SATURDAY
6:00	Restful Recharging of Batteries	Daily Motivation	Daily Motivation	Daily Motivation	Daily Motivation	Daily Motivation	Restful Recharging of Batteries
7:00		Leading by example workout	Leading by example workout	Leading by example workout	Leading by example workout	Leading by example workout	
8:00	Leading by example workout	Purposeful Commute	Purposeful Commute	Purposeful Commute	Purposeful Commute	Purposeful Commute	
9:00		Insuring Financial Stability for My Family	Insuring Financial Stability for My Family	Insuring Financial Stability for My Family	Insuring Financial Stability for My Family	Insuring Financial Stability for My Family	Loving Time with Kids
10:00	Spiritual Enlightenment						
11:00	Loving Time with Family						
12:00							
1:00	Healthy Body Replenishment	Healthy Body Replenishment	Healthy Body Replenishment	Healthy Body Replenishment	Healthy Body Replenishment	Healthy Body Replenishment	Healthy Body Replenishment
2:00	Buddy Time						Devotion to Honey Pursuits
3:00							

4:00	Keeping House Tip Top						Keeping House Tip Top
5:00							
6:00		Purposeful Commute – Me Time	Purposeful Commute – Me Time	Purposeful Commute – Me Time	Purposeful Commute – Me Time	Purposeful Commute – Me Time	
7:00		Loving Time with Family	Loving Time with Family	Loving Time with Family	Loving Time with Family	Loving Time with Family	Loving Time with Family
8:00	Kickback Time	Buddy Time	Keeping House Tip Top	Personal Pursuits — Me Time	Personal Pursuits — Me Time	Hot Date with Honey	Family Night
9:00							
10:00			Honey Time	Honey Time	Honey Time		
11:00	Restful Recharging of Batteries	Restful Recharging of Batteries	Restful Recharging of Batteries	Restful Recharging of Batteries	Restful Recharging of Batteries	Restful Recharging of Batteries	Restful Recharging of Batteries

think of in the color and subject line. What a great feeling. I love it! The kinesthetic might also be achieved by using language like *whipping the house in shape* in the body of my planner where I detail the task.

The combination of all three of these sensory inputs makes my schedule description strong and inviting to me. Even more satisfying would be technology that allowed for smells—in this case, the clean smell of Pine-Sol or a lavender vacuum bag insert, for instance—and touch, like soft, fuzzy feeling of a freshly vacuumed carpet. But for now, we'll work with what we have. It's still pretty effective.

Now that I've covered the mechanics of how to describe things on your schedule, next we're going to tackle *why* you decide what activities to put in your schedule.

TIME ISN'T THE PROBLEM TAKEAWAYS:

1. Here is one activity from my schedule…and this is the VAK.
2. VAK is important to me in this way.
3. Who benefits most from this activity? How?
4. I could really benefit when I deliver more on my schedule for success. I would be better off in these ways.
5. These are the actions I will take right now that will eliminate the things distracting me from delivering on my schedule for success.

STRATEGY TWO

PURPOSE

WHY YOU DO WHAT YOU DO

Focus = Meaning = Emotion = Decision = Action
—**Tony Robbins**

Okay. I hope you now understand and appreciate the importance of language. You might even have been amused by my choices of words for the roles in my life or the colors I use for them in my schedule. Armed with this new information you might even have come up with a few names for the roles in your life. So you're home free, right?

Uh, not so fast. How do you really know if the names you thought up for roles are really the right names for you, the most powerful terms you can use to help motivate you into completing your tasks?

That's where the next area of focus comes in. This next section deals with some really heavy subjects and is sure to get you thinking in ways you may not have up to this point in your life. That's a good thing.

It's always a good thing when we get the chance to stretch our brains. Soooo, take a deep breath, relax, and turn your mind to the on position.

We're talking values and beliefs here.

- How do we value things?
- What rules do we use to define those values?
- What are our beliefs?

Heavy questions, yes. But I'm not asking you to rethink your entire life. Often the changes needed to make a difference in life are not that monumental. I like to call them tweaks. A change in how you express things, a change in how you define situations, a change in how you feel, a change in focus. Any movement can have an expediential effect on your life if you take action to make it happen.

THE FEAR FACTOR

> *"The industrial age brought material prosperity that eliminated a lot of the natural challenges life used to deliver— but it also brought obesity, poor health, lack of purposeful existence, and a general malaise with an alarmingly large percentage of the population in dependency."*
>
> —**Mark Divine**

However, like I said earlier, most people resist change. Even when people are stuck in situations they don't like, they resist change. Why? The answer is simple: FEAR.

But what is fear, really? Terror? Dread? Anxiety?

The answer is: No! When I say fear, I mean fear by its true definition: *False Emotion Appearing Real.* Fear is the only thing in the world that gets smaller when you run toward it. But most people's instincts are to run as far away from fear as possible—and that's when the real trouble sets in.

Let's break down that word *fear*. Something that's false—meaning not true—appearing real. How many hours, days, weeks, even years, are wasted on thinking about something that's not real and isn't happening?

Danger is very real. Fear is not. Fear arises when the mind says, "Stop this is going to hurt", and we listen, even though this thing that our mind says is going to hurt hasn't happened yet.

Can the mind predict the future? No, it can't. But because, subconsciously, we believe it can, we let fear control us. Courage comes when we face this fear and make the choice to ignore it, and in doing so, change the future. The thing that scares us the most is the thing we most should be doing. As Eleanor Roosevelt said: *Do one thing every day that scares you.*

How can you change the story your mind is telling you? The answer is to use language that is empowering rather than disempowering, and by adjusting your strategy, your story, and your state. Ask yourself if what before you is a real danger or merely something your mind is telling you to fear. If the danger is real, then you need to address your strategy and your state. For example, if you're driving a car and about to have a collision, you would adjust your strategy by turning the steering wheel to go where you want to go and focusing on avoiding hitting whatever's in your way.

If you're dealing with fear—False Emotions Appearing Real— the first thing you want to adjust is the story you're telling yourself. The best way to come up with an empowering new story is to change your focus and language, you know, your state. Once you do that, you can adjust or modify your strategy.

Here's are some examples of what I mean.

You might have a fear of snakes. But the odds of coming across a snake in, say, your own living room, are slim to none. Therefore, being afraid of snakes meets this definition of fear—false emotions appearing real. The probability or risk of danger is non-existent.

Another example would be a person who is afraid of vampires. To my best knowledge, you're not going to find a vampire in your back yard—or anyplace else I'm aware of.

In both of these cases, you're making up a story about the possibility of danger, and in order to get rid of this false fear, you've got to change the story you've told yourself about this false fear.

However, danger is very real, and it's important to make the distinction between danger and false fear. Your job here is to come up with a strategy to deal with the circumstance and take that action. If you're camping out in a rain forest, there is a real possibility you might encounter a snake or something equally icky, like scorpions. Therefore, in that instance it's entirely justifiable to be prudent and shake out a towel before using it, to make sure it's scorpion free. That's acting out of the fear of genuine danger. There's no need to change your story about this. The scorpion is something to be feared, and if you've ever come face to face with one, you know exactly what I mean.

The point is simple. Whenever you find yourself facing a fear, look it in the eye and ask yourself if what's in front of you is a real danger or just a story you've talked yourself into believing.

EVERYBODY HAS THESE NEEDS

Too often we let distractions run our lives. There are a couple of reasons for that. One is because of the way an action does or doesn't meet our needs. When we have great intentions to say, "I know I should and really want to do this but I'm not," it's because we're competing with something else that is vying for that time. At the moment, that other thing that distracts us, feels better.

Here's what I mean. On your way to the gym you pass by a donut shop. If you really like donuts, the idea of eating a bunch of those doughy delights feels satisfying. You decide to stop and go inside. Standing there, that sugary smell really excites your olfactory system, and just looking at those racks of glazed and jelly donuts make your mouth water. On an intellectual level you know they're not healthy, but you decide to buy half a dozen and end up eating three of them before you get back to your car.

Why did you go against your better judgment and stuff your face with junk? Because in the moment doing so felt great and satisfied a need.

Once you get in the car, however, guilt sets in, because you know that eating the donuts defeats the purpose of going to the gym. While going to the gym doesn't always feel like a fun time, you know it's valuable and the tighter abs and less flab is ultimately worthwhile. But that result takes time. You don't go to the gym just one time, work out and proclaim, "I'm there, and I'm done." Fitness takes time, discipline, commitment, and patience.

Now here's where language fits into all this. Let's say on your calendar you call this exercise time *workout.* As I've demonstrated earlier, workout is a limp word...and even has the word "work" in it. How much fun can that be? That word clearly will not meet any of your needs at a high level.

What you need is a different, more empowering way, of looking at the situation. How can you make that juicy? How can you spice that up? How can you use language that's supporting the experience that you want?

You figure that out by coming to realize that what you really, really need is to have a life that matters. What are the components of such a life? Doing things that satisfy one or more of your basic human needs.

What are your basic human needs? Abraham Maslow, Tony Robbins and David Hawkins have all written about these critical urges that control our behavior. They include the following:

BASIC HUMAN NEEDS			
Acknowledgment	Appreciation	Authenticity	Awareness
Beauty	Being heard	Choice	Comfort
Contribution	Creativity	Family	Food
Freedom	Friendship	Goals	Growth
Healing	Honesty	Independence	Individuality
Love	Mastery	Meaning	Mourning
Movement	Passion	Peace	Play
Protection	Respect	Rest	Safety
Self-worth	Sex	Shelter	Stability
Support	Teaching	Touch	Trust
Understanding	Warmth/caring		

For the purposes of transforming your life from stress to success, I believe these six are the most relevant:

Sureness
Uncertainty/Variety
Substance
Love and Connection
Stretch/Growth
Contribution beyond ourselves

Let's take a look at them in detail.

SURENESS AND UNCERTAINTY/VARIETY

I've combined these two needs here because everyone's balance of these is different and no one balance is better than the other. For instance, I'm a risk taker, and as such, I need more variety in my life then I need sureness. If I had to do the same thing day in day out all the time, I'd be bored out of my mind. But others crave routine, and would feel lost if they had to continually recreate their schedules. The certainty of the routine is comforting. That's why the regimen of military life appeals to many, and why, ultimately, I concluded that the life of a Marine was not for me.

In our workout example, sureness can show up in several ways. One is if you know it's going to hurt to work out, you're going to be reluctant to start. Not much opportunity for fitness success with this mindset. However, if you go into a session with the assuredness that all those push-ups and bench presses are going to help you lose those love handles, thighs, or growing extra chin, you're going to be more motivated to keep at your routine.

Uncertainty/Variety can work both ways too. If you go to the same gym, the same time, do the same workout, with the same people, there's not a lot of variety, and you're likely to get bored. However, if you conscientiously make sure to keep mixing up your exercise regimen, you'll be more motivated to keep working toward your goal.

LOVE/CONNECTION

Love and connection are critical to everyone. We all want to feel connected. We all want to feel we have the ability to love others. For instance, I reserve my deep love for my wife and my son, and love for the rest of my family.

Often, however, we don't or can't find that love, or we'd all be singing *Kumbaya* all the time. It's also why we sometimes settle for connection. We find it easier and less painful to have a superfluous connection with some people.

Let's face it; we don't want to love everybody. I don't want to love all my co-workers, people that I go out to a restaurant with, or casual acquaintances. I want to have a connection with them, and I want this relationship to be sincere. But I don't want to have an intimate love with everyone. Therefore, we have connection.

Often what happens is – and this is where Facebook or whatever social media flavor of the year can become an addiction and a problem – we will settle for connection because it's safer than real love. This is why people will have hundreds of connections on Facebook and not even know who their neighbor is.

We might shy away from love because of the fear that somebody might hurt us, or we're going to hurt them. As great as our intentions may be, there's often as much pain associated with love as there is joy. Ideally, you want to have more joy, fulfillment, and compassion than pain, but things don't always work out that way.

This is why a lot of people will avoid love. It's also partly why people stay in an unsatisfying career, unhappy marriage, or relationship.

In our workout example, there's probably not much love and connection when you work out by yourself. But the act of getting in shape may make you feel more love for yourself, and that *is* to your benefit.

SUBSTANCE

Next up is substance. We all want to feel important, needed, and wanted in our lives. We want to know that we matter. It is how we act that makes us unique. It's the difference between someone who gets their importance by doing and being, versus someone who gets their importance by playing up their role as the victim.

This is why you could have somebody who gets his substance from being a kamikaze pilot or a terrorist. Or to be somebody like Gandhi or Mother Teresa, somebody who has really made an impact on others in the world.

Most of us look to find being enough on a smaller scale. We do that through our careers, our roles in relationships with a spouse or a child or a friend, our faith-based affiliation, or a host of other situations.

You have an opportunity to add substance to your life by making choices, setting a course of action, and putting it on a calendar and on a schedule. It's not that difficult.

Back to the workout example. If you believe everyone at the gym is in great shape, that they're doing more weights, more reps, or exercises or routines you can't do, you will feel inadequate and less likely to go. However, if leading a workout in a group fills you with a sense of community and pride, that you're all there together for the greater good, there's substance and being needed in that feeling. This could prompt you to continue showing up again and again.

STRETCH/GROWTH

If you can have those four needs fulfilled, you will most likely feel satisfied and have happiness in your life. Most of the time. Most people can live successful and productive lives by embodying those four vital needs. However, I don't see you as one of these ordinary people. I believe you're extraordinary—or at least striving to be extraordinary. I believe if you want those needs to sustain themselves over time, you also must also choose to add growth and stretching into your life.

To me, stretching is pretty self-explanatory. Grow or you shall die.

A stretching capability can be measured in personal development. One example of stretching is learning how to play a musical instrument. You can certainly go through life without ever knowing which end of a trumpet is up, but anyone who has learned the language of music will attest to the positive benefits that knowledge has had in other aspects of their lives.

In a relationship, growth comes from learning how to enhance, evolve and develop beyond your current capability. Growth can also be educational, emotional, or financial. But you must continue to grow.

Need a visual to truly understand this concept? Here it goes. A stagnant pond is not a pretty place to want to be around, is it? It's infested with mosquitos, smells bad, and is full of nasty decaying rot. Obviously this is a bit of an extreme example, but our lives operate pretty much the same way. Often we don't notice that we've stopped growing and that our lives have devolved into a stinky stagnant unappealing stench. Growth gets thwarted or impeded when we get comfortable. Comfortable is a great place to visit but you don't want to live there because complacency keeps us small and unmotivated to pursue our dreams.

I've come to realize my number one need is not love, it is growth. I'm constantly looking for ways to learn, to get new, to understand, and to go deeper.

In our workout example, if you stay on your regimen, you're exhibiting growth.

CONTRIBUTION BEYOND OURSELVES

In order to be truly fulfilled we need growth and we need to contribute beyond ourselves. This shows up in our relationships with other people. Long term fulfillment comes through the act of contribution

When most people here the word *contribution*, they get frozen in their tracks. In their heads they're thinking this means they have to jump on the next plane to Africa to fight Ebola, open up a soup kitchen in their local distressed area or organize a fund raiser to save the whales. While people who contribute on this macro level are to be applauded and admired, don't feel bad if you don't feel called to do anything equal to that or parallel. You can play a powerful role in others' lives by contributing on a micro level. This means doing things in your everyday life that create a positive affect for those around you. This can be something as simple as buying a bag of gummy bears for your kid, making the bed for your spouse, or holding the door open at your office building. These actions matter too, maybe even more because they affect those closest to you.

Contribution to others is very important for me. That's why I have such a passion for psychology, became a professional life coach, and got involved in charitable projects.

My personal order of needs is growth, contribution, love, substance, variety, and sureness. Sureness is the last thing on my plate because I don't need a whole lot of safety or security to try something. I believe risk taking for me results in a higher quality—and often more successful—life.

If sureness is number one on somebody's list, they require discomfort to be nearly nonexistent or they aren't going forward. This is one of the reasons why a lot of people don't take action. Their inability to step out of their comfort zone holds them back from achieving what they really want.

Can this be changed? Can sureness get pushed lower down on the list in these people? The answer is yes, and we'll explore how in the coming chapters.

TIME ISN'T THE PROBLEM TAKEAWAYS:

1. This is something I am afraid of. I can reframe that F.E.A.R. like this.
2. My six human needs are ordered in this way, for these reasons.
3. In living a life that truly matters, I would imagine seeing the six human needs ordered like this.

THE BUILDING BLOCKS OF LIFE

If you're a person who craves sureness above all, it's going to be very hard to make changes, such as taking action in career, relationships, or anything else. Your need for sureness created the story of your life around this key belief. The story says this is who you are, this is how you behave, and why you take the actions you do or make the decisions you make.

You're not alone. We've all created the great, powerful stories than run our lives. They determine our state and how we show up. Do we show up fluid and flexible, or do we show up rigid, shallow-breathing and all bound up? What are we focusing on? How do we transform from here to there?

- *What do I find myself continually thinking about when I'm in the shower?*

First, I offer you to look at the story that you started with.

- Do you like it?
- Do you like the state this puts you in?
- What words are you using to describe this?
- Do these words help make this story a resource or a problem?

As an example, let's say you're working as an employee in a company. You're dissatisfied being there. For whatever reasons, the job has become a chore, and you consider five p.m. on Fridays as the happiest time of the week.

You've thought long and hard about your plight and daydream about opening your own business, where you make the rules and control your destiny. However, the security of your paycheck and vested 401K, and your need for the sureness of this money for your survival, keeps you tied to the drudgery. That, and the uncertainty of what it takes to be a successful entrepreneur, will keep you in your unhappy yet familiar comfort zone.

Or let's say you've moved beyond this point and are ready to retire. You've planned well and have a tidy nest egg that could keep you in your standard of living for as long as you want. But you're so wrapped up in the story that you are your job, that you can't imagine life without working. There's a part of you that actually believes that once you stop working you will lose your entire identity and no one will want to be around you. You deny yourself the pleasures of what retirement could offer because you don't want to jeopardize the comfort of your present situation.

This chart helps illustrate some other ways how the stories we tell ourselves impede us from following our dreams.

HOW OUR STORIES MAKE US MISERABLE			
GOAL	STORY	OUTCOME	WHAT YOU'RE MISSING
Being a comedian	Audience won't laugh	Never try	Satisfaction of fulfilling a passion, bringing joy to others
Traveling abroad	Fear of getting sick, terrorism attacks, high cost	Never travel	Joy of seeing the world, having stories, and the variety of good surprises
Skydiving	Parachute won't open	Never try	Freedom of floating in air; Fly like a bird
Writing a book	Nobody will read it	Never write it	Joy of self-expression
Marriage	Afraid no one will love me	Loneliness	Happiness of living life with a partner

- *What would I do if I knew I couldn't fail?*

Chances are if you're unhappy with your life direction, your story is holding you back. One way to analyze your story is to realize that people tend to be in one of four stages of conflict. These stages can be looked at like a pyramid, with the largest, most common stage at the base. That stage is survival. Coming next is stability. The third stage is success, followed finally by significance. Let's take a look at those stages in detail.

SURVIVAL

> *"Isn't providing for your family enough motivation to do the things you don't want to do?" No, because it's easier to adjust to the hardships of a poor living than it is to adjust to the hardships of making a better one!"*
>
> **—Albert E. Gray**

The first foundation stage, or the very bottom, is survival. It's at the bottom because it's the stage in which, oh conservatively speaking, I'd say about ninety-seven percent of us live. Not only is this where we start, but we can't reach the later stages, success and significance, until we master our way out. You cannot live in survival and make decisions for success without dropping back down, because without learning how to master stability, any success that's achieved is not going to last. One event that knocks you off your feet could tumble you back into survival mode.

A lot of people live their lives like this. They have periods when things are going great. They tell themselves they don't have to worry about survival anymore. They consider themselves stable and they get comfortable in that feeling.

But then something happens—a lost job, an illness, a broken relationship—that causes them to come back down into survival. Survival mode often doesn't feel right. It's exhausting and ultimately self-sabotaging. Yet because this is a known feeling and something we understand, there's also a bit of a comfort factor here. We feel safer with the familiar than we do with the unknown, even if this does sometimes leave a bitter taste in the mouth.

Nevertheless, the goal is to move up from survival to the next step, stability, and stay there.

STABILITY

Stability is achievable. There's a formula on how you can get there. It does take three things: discipline, persistence, and time.

If you have a compelling enough vision or meaning behind what you seek to do, you won't require a great deal of struggle for success. The inspiration of that purpose will drive you to do what you need to do! When you are stable, you have the self-awareness to choose what you want to bring into your life and what things you choose not to have in your life at this point in time. This doesn't mean that you're preventing them from ever coming in; it's just that right now you're being deliberate in your choices. This becomes very important and very essential and enables you to live a life that matters when this stuff becomes addictive and you start thinking this way.

I consider myself stable today because I have a daily and weekly formula that allows me to plan out a life of great experience. This allows me to be flexible, too, in being able to move things around in my schedule, without stressing me out and making me feel overwhelmed or out of control.

The key to achieving stability is planning and habits. That means that you want to map out where you're going and not just live your life on a whim. You want to build habits and practices to enable you to meet your goals. By doing this, when an event comes in that you need to get done, your mind is not playing the old habits of, "I didn't do this, why do I have to do this? I didn't even create this"; or "My boss this or that"; or "My spouse this or that." You tell yourself instead, "Wait a minute, I've got a choice here, and I get to look at this differently."

- *What's going on in my life currently that I could look at from a perspective of having choices?*

In the last section of the book, I'll discuss practical ways to put this formula into use. For now, it's enough to know that once stability becomes a steady part of your life, the next two parts of the pyramid fall into place.

SUCCESS

> *The world is full of people that have stopped listening to themselves or have listened only to their neighbors to learn what they ought to do, how they ought to behave, and what the values are they should be living for.*
>
> **—Joseph Campbell**

I define success as that which is meaningful to me. Meeting my standards, not society's standards. Success is achieved when you have good habits and execute on those habits to achieve your objectives repeatedly. Success is a level of conscious competence where you have a formula or plan that you can follow each time and expect to achieve the same reasonable success each time. Think of it as a flight plan knowing where you currently are, where you want to be, and a route mapped out how to get there. In fact, you may be entering the stages of unconscious competence or "mastery" where your habits no longer require deliberate thought but are wired so tightly that you can unconsciously achieve your objectives.

This is like learning to drive a manual transmission automobile. Remember the first time you tried to operate this vehicle? If it was anything like my experience, it was ugly. Step 1, push in the clutch. Step 2, release foot off the gas the instant you depress the clutch. Step

3, shift the transmission into new gear… and on and on. The problem is, the first time you either stalled out or jolted and lurched that vehicle in some tragically comedic ways (well my brothers and sisters thought so anyhow). Eventually with repeated discipline and practice you have success doing this smoothly and reliably. Mastery is achieved when you can operate a manual transmission vehicle without having to think step 1, step 2, step 3, etc., but rather you operate the vehicle intuitively while having the capability to eat a sandwich, listen to music, and engage in a conversation… not that I recommend anything but hands at 10 and 2!

SIGNIFICANCE

Significance comes when your standards equals or exceed society's standards. This doesn't mean ego. This just means you have made an impact in one person's life or in your family's life or in your community's life or in the life of the world. It's when you've completed what you intended to do on whatever level you intended. Using the manual transmission example one more time, this is when you have the ability perhaps to excel at driving a race car exceptionally well while others cannot handle this level of difficulty. Your standards exceed that of most others in this case.

WHAT KIND OF TREE ARE YOU?

The Master Coach Peter J. Reding created a wonderful metaphor for self-examination that I'd like you to consider. Pretend you are a tree. Since we're talking about our own needs, let's call this the "Tree of Life." Most of us think we want to operate at the treetop, at the leaves. It's the fun place, the place that gets the sun and the rain and the refreshing breeze.

Let's say a storm comes in. What happens to your tree in the storm? Are you like a pine tree, with a shallow root structure? Or an oak tree with a tap root and a very strong, deep root structure.

If you're a pine tree, you're not going to handle things very well. Most likely you'll topple over, leaving your roots exposed. What if that represented your life? What if all of the things at the top of the tree were the material things or the to-dos you tell yourself: "If I get all of this then I win, then my life will be complete…once I have X amount of money, once I have this body, once I have this amount of time doing this or that, then I'll be complete."

You got it. That would be a life based on survival.

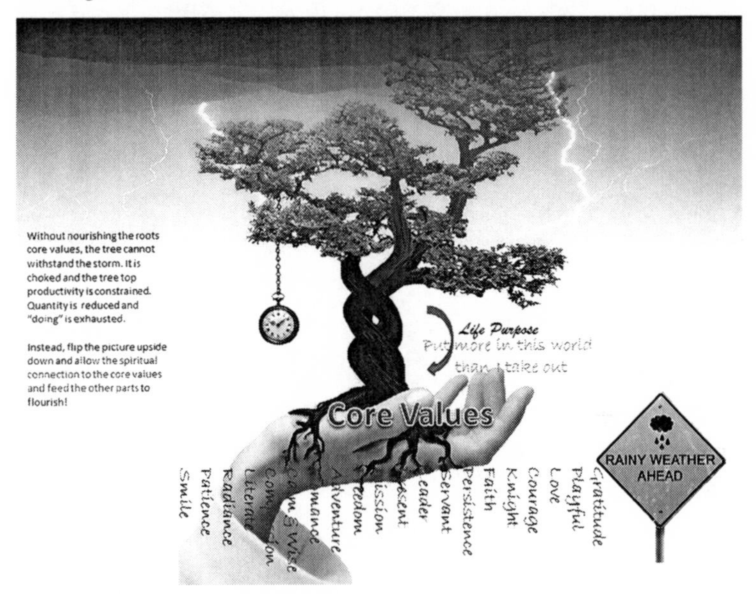

Find larger image online at www.ChadECooper.com

When you live a life focused on survival issues, the chances of toppling in a storm are greatly increased.

But what if your life were more like the oak? A life with a deep, strong root system is a life based on your core values; some examples of this may be compassion, love, generosity, and gratitude. When these values are held strong in your life, the chances of losing everything in a storm are greatly decreased. Sure, you may lose a branch or two, but you will have the strong base to lean on.

If we design our experiences by our values, then we know when the times are good, those experiences will be strong, powerful, and fulfilling. But if hard times come along and try to knock us over, because we're rooted in our deep core values, we will be resilient enough to weather the storm.

Perhaps you've never really taken the time to really figure out what your values are, whether you're more like the pine or the oak. Take time to do so now. If you discover you've been living like a pine and want to be an oak, there's time and opportunity to fix that.

A great example of how this works in everyday life can be seen in relationships. Let's say you have a spouse. What do you value in him/her? Compassion? Giving? Generosity? Love?

Now take a look at your schedule. How many of those values show up in the way that you're living out your week?

Are you doing things that show and represent the love – like doing the dishes, listening to their concerns, cleaning the house, giving that person a massage, getting him a new golf club, or sending him to some exotic, crazy, cool place? Are you there to show empathy and compassion if your spouse is faced with a troubling situation? Those are the values of the strong and mighty oak.

Contrast that with the actions of a pine tree, where instead of reacting with empathy, you might brush off your loved one by telling them you're too tired or stressed out to pay attention to them. Believe me, I've been there myself, and at the time, the story I told myself to justify my behavior felt reasonable and compelling in my head. Only in reflection afterwards did I realize I was selling my loved one—and myself—short.

Why do we do this? Because we are focused on the short-term gains at the tree top and at the moment our behavior feels good, but it's not good for us or for others. At the time we have to make a choice, we may feel that our core values don't feel good even though they're good for us. So we cave to temptation, ignoring the needs of others for our own short-term needs. When the storm attacks in the form of an argument, we tumble over because we haven't exercised the muscles of our values such as patience, compassion, love, respect, gentleness, etc., and instead react with defenses and deflection "Well, if you didn't first *insert the blank* then I wouldn't have *insert your poor decision*" and down the spiral we plunge.

This is important to know, because when something unpleasant or unforeseen happens, you know you're still solid and standing strong. However, if you haven't been paying attention to or honoring the values you hold dear in your spouse, when that rough patch happens, regret sets in. "Gosh, I wish that we had played more. Gee, I wished we'd spent more time together. I wish we'd taken more vacations." Often these regrets come too late, after the relationship has deteriorated to the point of no return. Yet with attention, persistence, commitment, and time, all could have been prevented and maybe still can be restored.

TIME ISN'T THE PROBLEM TAKEAWAYS:

1. I am here in the life pyramid. I like where I am, or I really want to be here instead.
2. I am this kind of tree because of these reasons. I like being this tree, or I would rather be this tree.
3. These are three values that are most important to me. I live them like this.
4. Look at the story that I started with. Do I like it? Do I like the state it puts me in? What words am I using to describe this? Do these words help make this story a resource or a problem? Considering this, I am rewriting it to empower me and ground me in my values.

UNLOCKING THE SECRET TO YOUR SUCCESS

"Destiny is no matter of chance, it's a matter of choice. It's not a thing to be waited for, it's a thing to be achieved."

—William Jennings Bryan

In the last two chapters, I told you all about the importance of knowing your basic needs. I hope you've given some thought as to the priority you give each one. You did do that, right? Good. Because these are the ingredients you need to help you define your purpose.

How important is it to really know your purpose? About as important as the air you breathe.

Why do I believe this? I've seen the proof. Clients have sought me out as a coach because they've been suffering from depression or been so unmotivated about life they believe they have no reason to get out of bed. What's the main reason behind this? Lack of purpose, resulting in guilt, or shame.

Even people who've achieved enough financial success to enable them to retire are not immune from this feeling. With them, the symptom shows up as illness. Many retirees get ill soon after they stop working because they're still looking for a purpose, and an illness gives them significance, connection, and variety; perhaps the same things their career gave them. You can argue whether that's why illness happens or not, but I believe lack of purpose makes you susceptible because people will use negative drama in order to get connection, in order to meet their needs.

If we aren't purposeful, if we don't know what our purpose is, then the Universe will make that decision for us. Most of the time that decision will be something unpleasant like depression or illness.

I often like to use the analogy of Murphy's Law—"anything that can go wrong will go wrong." I like to think of Mr. Murphy as a person who comes knocking on your door. If your house is in order, if you have purpose, he takes a look and goes, "Oh, I must have the wrong address," and he goes to your neighbors. But if your life is adrift, Mr. Murphy will keep coming back again and again.

Just like a doctor who needs to know the underlying cause of an illness to prescribe a treatment, you have to determine the underlying cause of your discontent if you want your life to be fulfilling. That means finding your purpose. Being without purpose leaves you adrift, and drifting can be a problem. You may feel as if you're out in limbo, because you are.

However, if you have a reason, a "why", and you have strength in that reason, you have a strong foundation, like the roots of that oak tree. Anything can stand on top of that and be able to withstand anything that hits it.

Having purpose means having a plan, or a strategy, that you execute with precision. If you know your purpose, congratulations, you can skip this chapter and move on to the next. (Although I strongly encourage you to stick around.) If you don't, then it's imperative that you take some time and answer this very, very important question: What do you really, really, really want? More importantly, WHY?

ANSWERING THOSE BIG QUESTIONS

Yes, those are big questions, perhaps the biggest ones you will ever have to answer. To help you, let me share several stories that may give you guidance.

The first is the tale of two lumberjacks, a story first told by Steven Covey, author of the seminal work on human behavior *The 7 Habits of Highly Effective People*. Lumberjack A starts off his day with his mighty axe in hand and begins chopping wood. Periodically throughout the day he takes pauses and breaks. Lumberjack B starts off his day in the same way, only he's bound and determined to chop all day without a break.

At the end of the day, Lumberjack A has more wood chopped than Lumberjack B.

Lumberjack B is dumbfounded. "Excuse me," he says to Lumberjack A. "How could you have more wood chopped than me when you kept on taking breaks all day?"

Lumberjack A responds, "I wasn't taking breaks. I was sharpening my axe."

Having purpose, creating a plan, is about sharpening your proverbial axe. Working hard in and of itself isn't enough if there's no purpose there. Working smart, as Lumberjack A did, with planning and precision, will always yield more improved results.

The second story is about a man who walks into a hardware store to buy a box of nails and a hammer. He doesn't really want the nails or hammer. He wants to put a hole in the wall. He doesn't really want to drill to put a hole in the wall, he wants a nail in the wall. He doesn't really want a nail in the wall; he wants to hang a picture on the wall. He doesn't really want a picture on the wall; he wants the experience and emotions he receives when he looks at the picture on the wall.

Too often we fill our life with the distractions of the to-dos instead of the real outcome or the emotion we want in our lives. Which person do you want to be? The person who takes joy in looking at the picture on the wall or the person who spends so much time worrying and fretting about the process that all the enjoyment gets taken out of the experience?

PLANNING FOR RETIREMENT

When I was nineteen years old, I didn't know I was going to retire at age thirty-five. But I did start putting a plan into place at that young age. That's because I knew then that one of my goals was to be financially independent. I planned throughout my twenties—putting away some money in a systematic way—and when I got into my early thirties and close to my intended goal I started to get doubts. The economic collapse was on the horizon, and I was worried this was going to throw a wrench in my plans.

I made the determination to reframe my road to retirement as a two-year journey that I would tackle in pieces. I stayed on my job and was able to make additional money (working smarter, and yes harder), which I methodically put into savings. At the same time, I cut back on expenses to enable my family to live on less and less. By the end of those two years, I phased out my income altogether.

Now when your income goes from one hundred down to zero you're going to feel that. But because I had planned carefully, I had enough in the bank to ensure that, financially speaking, I could afford to retire in a way where I didn't feel the pain associated from no longer bringing home a regular paycheck. In reality, in order to truly retire, I do not include my wife's career in the equation. It just happens to be the icing on the cake so to speak. Can I walk away right now? Yes, does my wife's career allow us to not have to draw down on that savings currently? Yes.

But without her, I'd still be comfortable. My only expense is healthcare really which is insane (we won't go there). So for that reason, I am not including my spouse's income. So you might think "Ah HA! I knew it, he's not REALLY able to walk away!" When in reality I truly DID retire, not in the generic manner however; and that's what I want to emphasize! I want people to stop thinking of the same old stories, and create their own. Many people think retirement is some airy fairy role of hitting the golf ball around 4 days a week. Kill me if I ever do that before age 70, I am not a big golfer and certainly not more than 9 holes typically. In reality retirement for nearly everyone is about doing what you want to do on your timeframe. That's what I'm doing. If I had a billion dollars, I'd be doing exactly what I'm doing right now. Why? Because it's making a difference and it's on my terms instead of someone else telling me what to do, when to do it, and how. That's real freedom in my opinion.

What also helped me was patience and persistence. I realized that if I just concentrated on those pebbles—the day-to-day implementation of my plan—with time they would stack up to create the boulder that was my retirement.

Too often, though, people struggle. They work until retirement age, till the day they qualify to collect their pension, or start taking distributions from the 401K plan, or sign up for Social Security. They think a lot about that day the closer it approaches, filled with hope and anticipation, and excitement about giving up the daily grind.

Only one problem. They haven't stopped to find the solution to the question: Now what?

I am reminded here of the quote from the Dalai Lama about life. When he was asked what most surprised him about humanity, he said: man. "Man sacrifices his health in order to make money. Then he sacrifices money to recuperate his health. Then he is so anxious about the future that he does not enjoy the present; the result being that he does not live in the present or the future. He lives as if he is never going to die, and then dies having never really lived."

The hobbies that amused a lot of people as diversions while they were working become boring when they become the main activities of the day. Some may wind up going back to work just for something productive to do, while at the same time hating the experience because it's not what they had expected from retirement. They go back to what they know, whether what they know is healthy for them or not.

Retirement doesn't have to go like this. Studies have shown that the three most sought after post retirement goals are travel, more time with a spouse, and time for hobbies. Are any of these on your list? With the right planning and attention to your true desires, you can make your retirement years the best part of your life. Finally, you will have the time and the wherewithal to do the things you really want to do, but if—and only if—you take the time beforehand to really define your purpose.

TIME ISN'T THE PROBLEM TAKEAWAYS:

1. I can't fail, I'm not judged, and money is not a factor. Pretending that dream is a reality, I would be doing this. I would be this. I was born to be this.
2. These are the steps I am taking to create a viable retirement plan.
3. These are two realistic things I intend to do when I retire.

ROME WASN'T BUILT IN A DAY— NEITHER IS YOUR RETIREMENT PLAN

"Nothing in the world can take the place of persistence. Talent will not; nothing is more common than unsuccessful men with talent. Genius will not; unrewarded genius is almost a proverb. Education will not; the world is full of educated derelicts. Persistence and determination alone are omnipotent. The slogan 'Press On' has solved and always will solve the problems of the human race."

—Calvin Coolidge

I've never been a fan of New Year resolutions. In my opinion, these kinds of lists are often written down in the spur of the moment without any follow through. Often they end up hidden away in the back of a drawer, only to come out again the following December 31st, along with the inevitable sigh of regret at having seen a year go by without any results.

Resolution writing reminds me of a quote by Rabindranath Tagore: "*Regret spring is past, summer is gone, and winter is here and the song that I meant to sing remains unsung for I have spent my best hours stringing and unstringing my instrument.*"

So if New Year's Resolutions are your idea of a good time, I've got three words for you: STOP RIGHT NOW! They don't work.

I am a big fan of planning, however. Planning with purpose. Along with that comes the realization that anything worth planning takes time.

One of the most important items that everyone should plan out carefully is their retirement plan. Believe it or not, most people don't. Because they see retirement as a faraway thing, they keep it out of mind until one day they look at themselves in the mirror and realize all those gray hairs are never going to go away. (That is, if they're lucky enough to still have any hair on their head at all!) Then they take a look at their bank account and go into a panic.

You may be well into your working years, but that doesn't mean it's too late to create a retirement plan that's smart and most suited to your needs. It's never too late to start. The only mistake comes from not doing any planning at all.

We aren't just talking about financial planning. I know way too many retired people without a clue to what the day holds in terms of living their life's purpose. Before they retired, they were too busy working for survival and told themselves they didn't have time to think about what they really wanted out of life. Now that they're retired, they come up with the excuse that they're too old and about out of time. They're still alive yet ready to throw away their life without giving themselves to honor the reason they were put here on Earth in the first place.

How do you make a plan that's right for you? First, you have to take a deep breath and realize that it takes time. I didn't create my retirement plan from beginning to end in one long weekend. I just don't work that way. Neither do most successful people.

Neither should you.

My plan started out as snippets, pieces of ideas. I gathered them, one at a time, when inspiration hit. Over time, I created a whole stream of ideas. The next step was to find the flow and then take action consistently. The idea was not to focus on the goals, but to focus on the habits. That enabled me to go even further until the ideas coalesced into a plan.

> *"The individual who wants to reach the top… must appreciate the might and force of habit. He must be quick to break those habits that can break him and hasten to adopt those practices that will become the habits that help him achieve the success he desires"*
>
> **—J. Paul Getty**

CREATING FLOW THROUGH MIND MAPPING

What is mind mapping? It's a way of outlining ideas in a visual way, in order to grasp a greater understanding of a concept or project. In my case, I began my retirement mind map with the phrase "Living Life on My Timeline" which equaled *Retirement* in the middle. Then I added ideas and plans in categories that branched out from there. I put the pieces together to see how they connected, where they weaved and overlapped. I gave myself patience, the permission to allow myself time for the plan to come together.

I've included my mind map here as a guide. Warning: If you've never seen a mind map before, I remind you to not feel like you have to eat the elephant in one sitting!

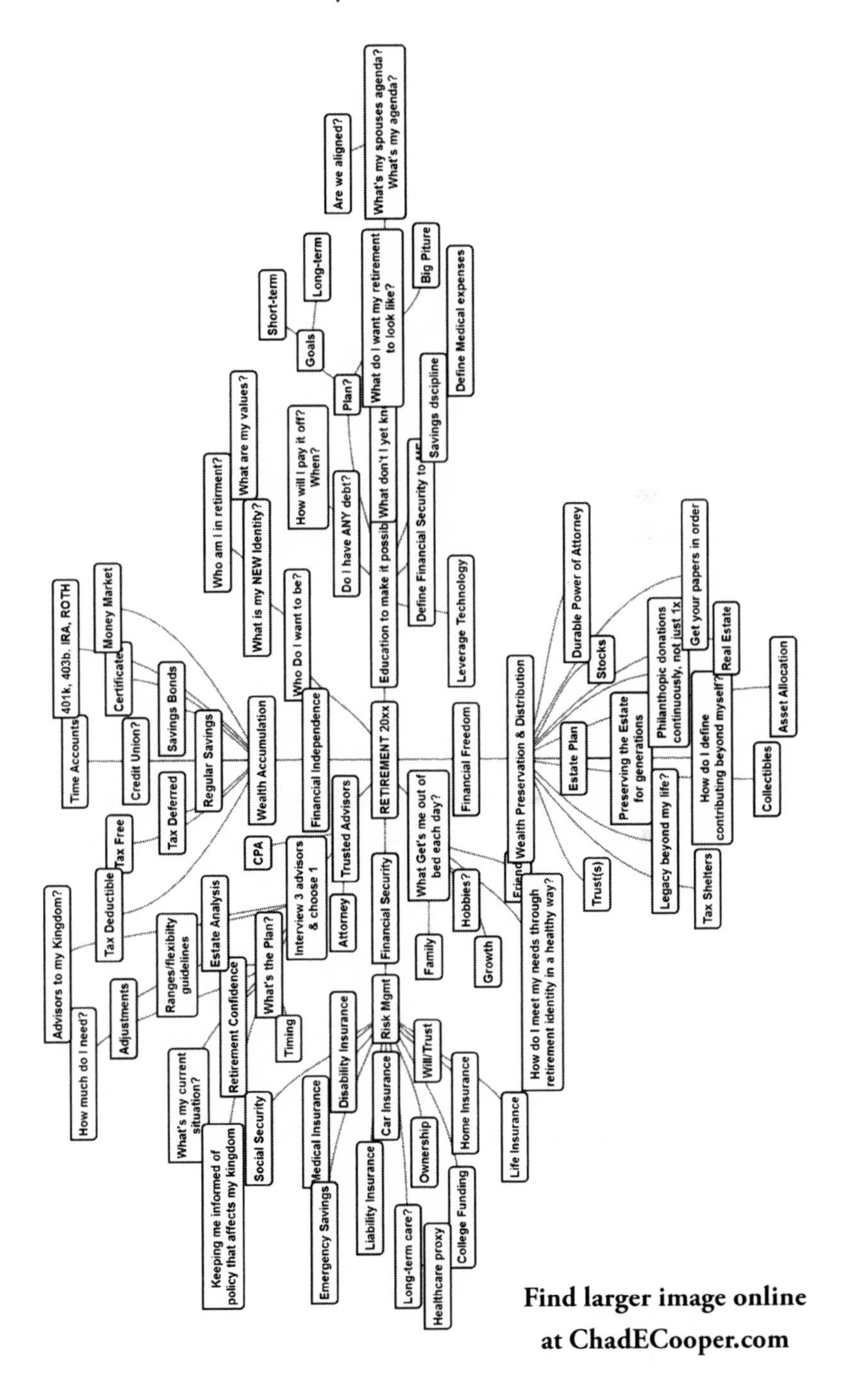

Find larger image online at ChadECooper.com

Those final pieces took a while to fall into place. I didn't panic or worry. I found that as long as I was passionate, as long as I remembered that I was on a journey and wanted to have fun while I was making progress, I was turning what could have been an arduous task into a game. I was creating an experience of *I get to do this,* not *I have to do this.*

Notice that in my mind map, I ask myself a lot of questions. That means that during this time, I did a lot of self-examination to figure out what I wanted and where my strengths and weaknesses were. I got to know my personality and realized that I'm what I would call failing "type-A recovery" individual.

Here's what I mean by that. Even though I liked the concept of being retired, I knew in my heart of hearts I couldn't stay retired in the traditional meaning of the word. Type A personalities are doers. We could be sitting on a beach on vacation and we'd feel compelled to be doing something—swimming in the water, reading a book, collecting shells on the beach. Even lying on a towel on the sand would be considered doing something, but only if the declared purpose was to get a suntan.

To ask a type-A person to *not* do something is like putting them in prison. To ask me not to do, would be asking me not to be. Therefore, I call myself a failing type-A personality—meaning I've given up on trying to suppress my overactive nature. I've tried to stay retired. But truth be told, I could never retire in the senior-citizen, 1950's model way most people look at retirement.

I had to keep active and involved. In my "retirement" I ended up creating new careers for myself. The result is that I now have three companies that I own and operate, which means I now live a schedule based on my plans, not based on an employer's demands. I learned enough about myself to realize I prefer being the owner versus the employee.

Now, I'm not saying that your retirement plan has to include your starting another career, like I did. No, my definition of retirement is really quite simple. It's doing what *you* want on *your timeframe*. It's taking your priorities and doing them in the way that you define. Retirement doesn't have to mean playing golf or poker or sitting in a rocking chair. Not that you might want to do those occasionally. But if you want to go on vacation or start another career or devote yourself to some other pursuit, you get to choose that.

Take a moment now and stop reading. Answer the following questions, which are similar to the questions I asked myself as I went through my process. Be as honest with yourself as you can. Remember, it's your life and your future we're talking about here! If you don't take a serious look at where you are and where you want to be, no one else will.

- *Which area best describes your financial state: Risk Management, Financial Accumulation, or Wealth Preservation?*
- *What are two actions you can take right now to move closer to your objective?*
- *Who do you want to be in retirement?*
- *What experiences do you want to have?*

THE NEED TO CONTRIBUTE

> *"Choose a job you love, and you will never have to work a day in your life"*
>
> **—Confucius**

I was very curious to know more about how people want to spend their time. In fact, I was so curious, I went out and paid money to have a study conducted to explore this. Not surprisingly, the top answers dealt with personal pursuits—taking vacations, spending more time with family and friends. I was surprised when the study showed that only four out of ten people want to contribute to others. In fact, it was only ranked sixth.

CHAD'S VALUES SURVEY

Looking at the following list, what are the TOP 3 things you'd like to spend more time with or more time doing?

Value	Percent	
Your children	33.7%	5
Your spouse or partner	48.2%	2
Contributing to your community	21.8%	6
Working	11.3%	
Pursuing your hobbies	39.5%	4
In spiritual practice	13.5%	
Managing your finances	10.3%	
Taking vacation	57.8%	1
Personal development (fitness, nutrition, meditation, etc.)	44.5%	3
Celebration	5.3%	
Other (please specify)	5.5%	

That's an important point, because in order for us to truly have fulfillment, we need to contribute to others. With this ranking so low in the results, it became clear to me why so many people feel as if they're missing something in their lives.

In my opinion, this is possibly one of the reasons why some of the most famous people in the world (like Janis Joplin, John Belushi, and Chris Farley) overdosed themselves with drugs. All the money in the world didn't buy them relief from their pain, or get them the happiness they desperately sought. They looked to drugs to give them the fulfillment and purpose they couldn't get any other way.

Okay, I can be wrong about this, but it's my opinion and I'm entitled to it. But I think I may be on to something here.

I discovered that my purpose in life is to put more into this world than I take out of it. This represents my mission and values.

I get to decide what that looks like, and one way I reinforce my commitment to this is through language. If I tell myself that doing service for others is going to be hard and time consuming, I might give up before I start. But if I tell myself it's a game and that I get to do something that puts smiles on people's faces, I'm much more likely to jump at the work with passion and enthusiasm. Again, that's my decision and choice.

Through my work as a Professional Life Coach, I have found that the quality of your life is based on how much you're willing to get outside of your comfort zone. Once you're able to move away just a little bit, you realize your hesitancy to take action was most likely based on false fear. Then when you take one step further out, your confidence rises and gives you the impetus to keep raising your standards. The next thing you know; you've created experiences that really matter.

If you're doing something you want to do with passion, and you use the empowering language to describe it, you will enjoy your efforts and have fun. You'll redefine the meaning of the word "work". You'll also be more likely to stay with your task to its completion.

I know. I know. You're probably saying to yourself, "Huh, easy for him to say. How do I know this will work for me?"

Truth is; I don't know if it'll work for you. I sure hope it does. All I can do is show you an example of how it has worked in my life.

I went through this thought process when making the decision to write this book. At first I felt resistance. Creating a book sounded like a lot of work, and who wants that? I was retired and financially secure, and more work was something I didn't need. I already had a full life with plenty to do. Additionally, when I really, really looked at myself, I realized I didn't know if I wanted to be judged by those who were sure to have opinions about what I had to say.

All of that could have been enough to stop me in my tracks before I started.

Then, I went back to the reasons why I came up with the idea for writing the book in the first place. I have a passion to put more into this world than I take out of it. I believe I've been blessed with gifts and talents that I can share with others, and that one of my gifts is to help inspire you to take action towards what you are most afraid of… how powerful you really are. If what I have to offer serves even one or two people, I will continue to give my life purpose.

Remember, the need to contribute is one of my most important needs. I knew I had to write this book...or else.

But first, I had to acknowledge that the old bugaboo fear was holding me back. I was worried about what others might think about what I had to say even before anything had come out of my brain. Talk about false emotions appearing real! I was putting non-existent words into non-existent people's mouths and letting that control my behavior. How crazy is that?

Once I realized I was playing these ridiculous mind games with myself, I was able to remember my purpose and told myself that if I just started with taking small steps, I'd have the courage and intention to continue moving forward until I finished this project. (Later in this book I'll detail how I fit this writing into an already full 168 hours.)

TIME ISN'T THE PROBLEM TAKEAWAYS:

1. These are the ways I'd like to make a difference in people's lives.
2. I want to contribute to others, and I currently may not be doing so to my standards. This is holding me back. What has to happen for me to feel successful in this area?
3. This action would make the biggest difference here, because of this.

YOUR PASSION IS YOUR OWN DAMN FAULT

If we continue to live by society's standards, we'll never be happy with what we have.

Here's a suggestion. Stop operating on the premise that you need to do things the way that everybody else thinks they should do things. That's fantasy thinking.

If we live by society's standards – it's a pretty low bar – we're going to end up having some problems. However, when you live by your standards and you implement them; your relationship with your spouse, your children, and your boss will improve. But most importantly your relationship with yourself will enable you to live a life that matters.

When you start subscribing to your own standards, you find they're likely a lot higher than what societies' are, and they're not as difficult to achieve as your fear makes it seem. **How you achieve them is represented by the subject line in your schedule.** Remember, language is key. Make that subject line as empowering as you can. Take heed of your VAK, and use language that describes the feelings you want, and the emotions you wish to convey to the world.

BE THE EXPLANATION, NOT THE EXCUSE

> *"The thing that scares us the most is the thing we most should be doing most."*
>
> —**Tiamo**

If you've stayed with me up till now, you've seen that I've accomplished a lot in my life so far. Here's the crazy truth about that. I haven't done anything that *anybody else can't do.* I didn't get here overnight. There's nothing special about me.

I didn't have all the happy Skittles®, puppies and rainbows background that some people think others always have. While I did have a happy childhood, I also experienced tragedies, and had my share of traumas. The difference is that, over time, I've learned to take some of those traumas, some of those unpleasant things that happened to me, and view them as an explanation and not an excuse.

What do I mean by that? Well, as an example, as I shared earlier, I enlisted in the Marine Corps. I distinctly remember one time, when I had the flu, and the Drill Instructor had a very creative and unique way of helping me with that illness; he had me do push-ups until I had complete muscle failure. TLC? Not in these barracks.

It was hard. It was difficult. In short, it sucked. In the end, "*sick me*" did push-ups for forty-five minutes. Up to that point, I thought there was no way I had the physical capability to do that. What I learned then was that the mind will tell you to stop when the pain begins, but that the body is capable is doing far more and going a lot further than that. It is up to us to decide when and whether to listen to our body or our mind.

As I mentioned in the introduction, I've had the privilege of doing the Ironman Triathlon; a 2.4-mile swim followed by a 112-mile century bike race followed by a 26.2-mile full marathon race. There is no logical reason for doing one. You have to have a lot of screws loose to put your body through that kind of abuse.

In order to succeed at such a rigorous event as a triathlon, you have to tell your mind, "Here's pain. It's part of this journey, and you're going to go along with me. But pain is not who I am."

If I had looked at the pain as an excuse and said, "Pain is who I am", I would have given up, and I would not have enjoyed my journey.

FOLLOW YOUR PASSION

The sooner you step away from your comfort zone; the sooner you'll realize that it really wasn't all that comfortable.

—Eddie Harris Jr.

When I was an undergrad in college, I had a double major in psychology and religion. At the time people asked, "Why would you want to study those? What do they have to do with each other?"

I'd answer, "People's rules and values go together. If I can understand the underlying reasons of what motivates people and their religious beliefs, what they value and stand behind, I can have a conversation and influence just about anyone anywhere."

Having a double major served me very well in learning about those relationships. Then, at graduation time, I had a very wise advisor who asked me, "Chad, you're about to graduate with these degrees, what are you going to do?"

I said, "I'm going to grad school and I'm going to become a psychiatrist."

She said, "Really? You got anything else in mind?"

At first I didn't understand the question. I didn't see what was wrong with my goal of being a psychiatrist. Since she was a wise advisor and I liked her, I gave her a thoughtful answer. My passion at the time was computers. Around that time the personal computer business was exploding, as a lot of people were buying desktop computers for home use.

I told her, "Yes, I've got five job offers for technology in the computer industry. But I'm going to be a psychiatrist."

"I'm just curious," she wondered. "What kind of salary are they offering you?" I told her the numbers the recruiters were dangling in front of me. "I love doing computers, but it's a hobby. It's just fun," I insisted.

"You really like computers?" she asked.

"Yes."

"If it's a hobby and fun," she said. "Would I be wrong to say you're passionate about computers?"

"I guess I am," I admitted. "Yes, I'm passionate about computers."

Then this advisor—I told you she was wise—gave me a bit of wisdom I cherish to this day. "Follow your passion," she said. "I can tell you, after fifteen years in this field, your entry salary in the computer field is more money than I'm making right now doing this job. Why don't you go have fun and make a lot of money at the same time?"

I followed this advice. I took a job with a computer company, entering into the world of the corporate environment. My mission was that if I was going to have a career, I was going to have fun and enjoy myself. If I ever got to the point where my passion was gone, it would be time for me to get out.

A lot of people would say, "That's a nice luxury that you have, most of us don't have that."

I say, "Really? Are you accepting what you get in life... or getting what you accept?" My belief is that if you take a job *for the money*, you end up paying for it with either boredom, unhappiness, dissatisfaction, or a general feeling that there's something missing.

If you live by the limp standard of accepting whatever comes your way; whatever you're given, and you say, "I guess that's as good as it gets," then, yes, you would subscribe to believing "I can't quit, it's not that easy." All the reasons why this path doesn't make financial sense or you've put all this time and mastery into this life choice.

I can understand that. But again, I've had some very intelligent and wise people say, "Chad, do you want to continue accepting what you get, or do you want to get what you accept?" My standard says that as long as I continue to get what I accept; I accept making my career fun, and passionate. I decided to live by this rule: *Follow your passion and work hard as much as you can, but if the passion dies, it's time to start looking elsewhere.*

In the early days of my corporate career, I had a lot of fun. Money was no object, parties were prevalent. We goofed off, yes, but we also worked hard, and because we were having fun, my time spent there was worthwhile and meaningful.

Then, the company culture started to change for me. Most of us have a hard time with change, and I was not immune to that.

I told you earlier about how I spent two years actively planning my retirement. Here is the reasoning behind the exact timing of my decision.

I realized I'd begun to lose my passion for the job when my last three bosses lacked… certain "people skills." The very last boss was—shall we say—deeply challenged. On the personal side, he was a great human being, but I believed he was promoted into a position above his skill level. He was unable to set priorities and manage effectively.

I felt as if I were put in an impossible situation. I tried to use all my talents and skill sets, but a typical conversation with him would go like this. "You asked me to do this and you asked me to do that. But there's only 168 hours in a week and you've asked me to do 190 hours' worth of work. Which of these two projects should I work on?"

"Do them both", he said.

Sighing deeply, I would say, "Let me go through this again. There's only 168 hours..."

He finally relented and would instruct me to concentrate on Project A. But then the next week he would call me into his office and say, "Stop working on Project A. Now I want you to do Project B."

This went on for a while. This incredible lack of direction made life painful for me. That's when I took a step back and asked myself that difficult question: What is my purpose?

This was a tough situation to face. Believe me, I had worked so long at this company that my career there was part of my identity. Without that identity, who was I? To make a change involved confronting my fears and caused me a lot of pain.

At the same time, I knew I had to do something. I was losing my passion for my work, and I knew in my heart—and in that one rule I'd created for myself—that when the passion was gone I had to make a change.

This was a scary place for me to go. It's a scary place for anyone to go. That's why most of us are afraid to go there. We usually end up continuing to do what we don't really want to do because we don't want to consider what else there is.

But that scary place I was facing wasn't danger; it was fear. Once I realized that, I was able to face my situation objectively. I concluded that this meant I needed a plan.

That's why I took two years. I knew I would have to face this challenge and create my plan one pebble at a time. I made a series of decisions. I asked myself the series of questions that were laid out on the mind map. Let me see what this might look like. Let me just start to live on a little less, and a little less.

If my identity wasn't in my career, what else was possible? What could I replace and become? I didn't have to figure all that out in one day. But over time I could.

Because I'd been careful with my money up to that point, I could see how I could possibly afford to be able to retire. However, the money was really just one part of the situation. I needed to know who I was. More importantly, who I could be, and who could I become.

The more I pondered these questions, the more the answer became very clear. *I could be absolutely anybody I want.* This enabled me to start imagining what the next phase of my life would be like, and then start making it happen.

TIME ISN'T THE PROBLEM TAKEAWAYS:

1. My calendar currently represents accepting what I get, and if not, am I intentionally designing it for the experiences I crave this week and getting what I accept?
2. This is a challenge I've had in my life where I responded as an explanation. How did I get through it?
3. This is an opportunity in my past where I am currently making excuses for my behavior today.
4. I can act as an explanation and be the cause of my future and not the effects of my past by doing these things.

LIFE IS NOT A HOLLYWOOD MOVIE

Fear is the only thing in the world that gets smaller when you run toward it.

I grew up with an alcoholic stepfather whom I loved dearly. Once, in a drunken state, he threw one of my brothers through a wall. This left a terrible impression on all of us that was very hard to accept.

Then, one day he gave up drinking. I grew to admire his courage and his willpower when he declared, "I'm not this anymore".

One late afternoon when we were on a family reunion together in the Georgian mountains, my stepfather and I decided to go for a walk down a gravel road. We wanted to get out after everyone was cooped up in the house from a fierce storm.

Trust me, if you've never been in the mountains of a country rainstorm, the experience of being on the same elevation as the storm is incredibly powerful and the ferocity of this event can really rock you.

The wind is piercing and the lighting truly lights up the sky because you are literally in the storm clouds. This had quite an impact on everyone, and we needed to shake off that feeling, so the two of us headed outside to see the effects along the road.

During a walk you usually begin talking about things as they arise and I wish I could say I had planned this moment, but sometimes like in that powerful storm, lightning strikes when you least expect it. I just blurted out, "There were some really crappy things that happened to us because of your behavior. But I have to tell you, I've never been more impressed than I am with you now. I've never seen the strength that a man can endure the way that I have seen you choose not to pick up another drink." I imagined how difficult that had to be for him, and I wanted him to see that I'd noticed.

At the time I didn't think this was a profound thing to say. I was just expressing my authentic feelings, but my admission forever impacted him. He went on to write some poems and letters that explained how much my words meant to him, how valuable he considered my encouragement and belief that he could be this other person he desired to be.

Unfortunately, his newfound take on life was much harder for the rest of my family, who still had too many hurtful memories from his earlier self, to forgive him. They couldn't understand how I could forgive him and, as a result, my brothers were upset at me for a period of time. They were especially mad that I had a more satisfying relationship with him than they did.

This was, however, an unspoken feeling that didn't get expressed until my stepfather died eight years after he had given up drinking.

"Why did you get to have that experience after he stopped drinking and he never gave us that opportunity?" they said to me at that time.

I said, "You guys got it backwards. He didn't give me that opportunity. I seized that opportunity. Just because I was the child didn't mean I couldn't suggest a change, a different relationship."

They hadn't realized that I had taken steps to mend that relationship by speaking from my heart. It was more important to me to accept my stepfather's past destructive behavior, forgive him for it, and move on to forge a new and closer bond, than to continue to resent him for old hurts.

I've also had other unpleasant tribulations. Growing up, I got yelled at by various authorities. I was teased as being a mama's boy, and as a result, had more than my share of fistfights with brothers. The difference is I don't live my painful memories. I might remember them and use them to help and inspire other people, but they don't define who I am.

I used my experiences as an explanation, not an excuse.

I don't know anyone who's lived a perfect life, free from traumas, hurts, or misfortunes. However, *how* you look at them makes a profound difference in the way you conduct your life. Awful things are events that happen to you. They're an explanation. But they're not an excuse to continue your non-supportive behaviors because of the past. They're not you.

If you keep using your low points as an excuse, they will prevent you from living a life that matters.

Yes, I have made mistakes, and, yes, I will continue to until the day I die. I might do things that hurt my wife or child or ruffle the feathers of my business associates. When I do, I don't wallow in it. If I make a mistake that causes hurt, I work to make amends, ask for forgiveness, and go on from there. I realize I'm just doing the best that I can.

My life is not like a Hollywood movie. Nobody's is really. But we can have some fun with the metaphor. What if you went to a movie theater to watch the story of your life? What scenes would you see? Are you the hero of your story? Are you the star of a farcical comedy? A three handkerchief weeper? A delightful romance? Or are you intent on your life being a tragedy with an unhappy ending?

Play around with the imagery. Have fun with it. Make your story have meaning and purpose. Then see where your imagination takes you.

TIME ISN'T THE PROBLEM TAKEAWAYS:

1. This is what I would see if I went to a movie of my current life right now. This is what I hear. This is how I feel.
2. This is what I see when I go to a movie of the life of my dreams!
3. This is how I need to be NOW in order to make this movie release in my life TODAY. This is what I am afraid of. If there were no limits, this would happen.
4. In one year, I want to remember these things.

STEP UP TO THE PLATE!

"What do I think about when I strike out? I think about hitting home runs."

—Babe Ruth

You want to see failure in action? Take a ride to a baseball field. I've had the honor and privilege of coaching Major League Baseball players, so I've gotten to really—get ready for the cliché—see the agony of defeat up close and personal. Professional baseball athletes, hitters in particular, are in an industry where failing seven out of ten times makes them one of the best. The only other place I can think of where those odds work in your favor is maybe being a meteorologist.

These men have picked this profession on purpose, choosing deliberately to have a career where failure is commonplace. Even reaching that level of success is very difficult. A Major League pitcher has to memorize and know the behaviors of an awful lot of opponents at bat. He also has to have the fortitude to deal with Major League fans who expect him to throw strikes every time, to wow *them*.

There's nothing I can teach professional Major League pitchers in talent and skill that they don't already know. They've gained that skill set in at least ten years of pitching in school and in the minor leagues before they ever show up in the majors. What do they struggle with? Why are some great and some others are not? They obviously have the mechanical talent to do what they do to get to that point. Why would they need a coach like me?

Because like everyone else, they live their stories. Ninety percent of what they do is about the story they put meaning to, in other words, what they choose to focus on. When the story is great, they're successful. As pitchers set up to pitch, they're thinking, "I've got to strike this guy out" or "Don't do this." They're focused hard on what they want, and they magnify, or amplify it, in their minds. As they look at this little thing, and as they keep looking and looking, the ball gets bigger and bigger. Or the ball starts small and keeps getting bigger and bigger until it becomes everything that they see.

This mindset holds true for hitters as well. It's not uncommon for star hitters to say that they see the baseball larger than life as it sails toward the plate. Some can even see the seams on the ball.

But these ballplayers are human, too. They're not always on top of their game. We've all heard of batting slumps, or the pitcher who suddenly can't seem to find the plate, for example. Sometimes a player will get so focused on what they **can't** do they want to quit, they want to stop.

That's where I come in. What I have learned to do with them is to remind them of their talent, where they are skilled, and how they got there. I remind them of the wonderful stories they've told themselves before. I have them look back to times in their lives when they were on the playground field with their buddies, when they just were out there having fun. Back then this game was truly a game.

One of the people I worked with was a pitcher who was on the downside of his career. Or so he thought. (I'm not going to tell you who he is, out of respect for his privacy, but believe me he's made a name for himself in the game.) His fear of failure started after he had a series of minor injuries that contributed to his losing a number of games. His coaches, believing he was overusing his arm, gave him some rest, but when he came back the magic seemed to be gone. He couldn't find the strike zone even if he were standing two feet in front of it.

Out of desperation or maybe inspiration, he hired me as his life coach. I had to find a way to get this guy back on track, so I took a look at the meaning he was giving to what was going on. Yep, it was that language thing again. He was saying things like he was "dreading" pitching against the league leading team at the time. He was staying out late the night before a game, telling himself it "didn't matter" whether he got a good night's sleep or not.

I got him to take a good hard look at his language. Yes, I started with his schedule. His language there was very poor, nothing more than the dates and the teams he was playing against. Can you imagine how inspired or excited he got when he looked at the schedule and saw, "Yankees, July 18th"? That's right, not much.

This was a far cry from the enthusiasm and love of the game he had back in his Little League days, when the thought of actually pitching against the Yankees would have seemed like the greatest dream come true. When I got him to realize that he was living his dream, in that he got to make money for doing what he loved more than anything else in the world, things started to turn around for him. He developed language that reinforced the idea that there was no concern about who won and lost, and that his passion was to throw the ball the best he could. He threw out the self-criticism that had been swirling his head, instead telling himself, "I'm enthusiastic, full of passion, curious, anxious to practice, and to refine my skills." He also started reminding himself to focus on one pitch at a time, rather than feeling the pressure of needing to strike out everyone he faced. He realized he didn't need to live by rules; he was just "being".

This pitcher remembered why he became a pro in the first place. Because he enjoyed the game. Because he loved the thrill of the action. Because he loved the challenge. Because he loved the satisfaction he got from performing.

He got rid of the limp language on his schedule and put in positive reminders such as "aim small, miss small" because as a pitcher his goal was to throw to a very precise area. He redefined sleep by calling it "fully recharged time". He also remembered to take time to celebrate. If he had a great workout, a strike out, or got out of a jam he would note it. By finding reasons to celebrate consistently, he continued to reinforce that positive psychology.

Finally, he created several roles he could take on. He came up with a special theme song that was played when he took the mound—a song that was designed to inspire him. When he felt the need to silence his inner, negative coach—that voice inside him that told him he had to perform—he became a combination of Nolan Ryan, Batman, and a Matador all in one. This allowed him to go back to the baseball field of his boyhood days, pitching one ball at a time.

The result? He became a winning pitcher again.

Our innate gifts are very much like those of professional athletes. Major League Baseball players don't go to the big leagues to strike out. They're there to hit home runs. Yet they don't let the strike outs affect them deeply. They know they can strike out seven times out of ten and still be considered one of the best in the world of what they do. This isn't about hitting grand slams every time. This isn't about perfection.

The idea is to try your best at every single moment. The thing I see the most killing a person is that they show up daily, go to the plate, and **bunt**! This is the equivalent of tossing your life away daily in little pieces. You can fail from time to time—and if you're a human being you will have failures in your life— and still have an incredibly abundant adventurous, fulfilling, passionate life.

But you have to show up with that passion front and center. Show up not content to reach first base on a walk, or even settle for getting there by getting hit by a pitch. It's about giving your all, facing up to life with the intention of hitting it out of the ballpark every time you try. If you don't, you get back up and you try again, because three out of ten times you're going to get a hit, and it's going to be incredible. The crowd is going to cheer and your fans are going to be there to celebrate that victory. It's that three out of ten times that brings the passion, that brings the juice, that makes you say, "I'm glad that I came up to bat, I'm glad that I went up there and gave it a shot."

TIME ISN'T THE PROBLEM TAKEAWAYS:

1. These are two challenges I've had to face in the past year. I handled them like this.
2. If I had to do them over, I would handle them like this.
3. These are two areas where I show up in my life and hit a home run each time.
4. These are two areas in my life where I am "bunting at bat". I will apply the values of the previous question toward these two areas like this.

THE WHEEL OF LIFE—
YOUR WHEEL OF FORTUNE

How can you balance your work life and your personal life? An effective way to help you visualize the answer to that question is a tool called "The Wheel of Life".

The Wheel of Life is not new. Lots of versions of this are available on the Internet. I've included one in the back of this book. Take a look at it now. As you can see, the wheel is cut into sections with each slice representing the different roles that each of us typically play on a regular basis. The center of the wheel is 0, and the very outer rim is a 10. You score yourself, category by category. It's important to note that you base your score on your standards not society's— because society would tell you that you need to be a 10 in everything.

The Wheel of Life can be seen as a visual proof of why time isn't the problem, you are. Time doesn't factor into the wheel. The wheel shows you where you think you stand in various aspects of your life—where you're satisfied and where you believe there's room for improvement.

Here's how I tell people to fill this out. I say if you think you're satisfied with how you're doing, rate it as 3. What that does is frame your mind into what you're doing right. But this also leaves room for improvement. If it's a category you're not happy with, mark this one lower.

Let's look at health, for example. If you're a 3 on health today and want to be a 5, what are you already doing well at a level 3? How are you doing a level 3 currently that honors you? Now what else can you do in addition to the 3 that would close the gap and allow you to reach 5? What specifically do you need to do to get there?

Then you can go around the whole wheel, one slice at a time. If this were a wheel on a car, how smooth of a ride would you have if you were going down a highway? Would this be a bumpy road or pretty smooth? When we are going slow and steady, as in our normal daily lives, it most likely doesn't feel too bumpy. However, when drama or difficulty emerges and things are going at a crazy pace that uncomfortable bumpy feeling turns into an uncontrollable vehicle about to crash!

Where do you need to round out this wheel and have the balance between personal and work life? Generally, people who are successful in their careers may be struggling in an area like health. They may be eating fast food or not taking time to work out because they're getting a lot of their needs fulfilled through their career.

One way to look for balance is to examine your week as a whole. Look at all of your roles and how much time you spend in each of them. Take *career* for one. Let's say you need to spend twenty percent or thirty percent of your week in that role. The first thing you should do is to change the language you use, using the methods described in Strategy One. Once you have really juicy language for all of them, especially the ones that don't really excite you, then look at where you're currently spending the percentage of your week. Where do you want to spend that time?

If you have those at a "7" then you can use that, and look at your schedule. How much time are you spending at that level currently? How much more time do you need to invest to get to the number you want to achieve? Then you can simply see where you can borrow that or leverage that from others areas, and then trade from those different slices. That way you will still have 100% of the pie, and you're not creating 110% in some imaginary way.

Let's say you want to get in tip-top shape, and in order to do so, you believe you should work out four days at half an hour each. That's two hours. Where can you take thirty minutes from all of those roles to get those two hours, or where can you take thirty minutes from several different roles to get those two hours? Maybe it's an hour of sleep one day a week, and maybe it's leaving work an extra hour early, or maybe it's cutting back and not doing a hobby for an hour one day a week. Perhaps it's simply getting up thirty minutes earlier four days a week?

What's it costing you not to do that? Is it worth borrowing from those in order to get over here? When you're in great health, how's that impacting how much focus, attention, presence and energy you bring to the other roles. I'm going to bet you show up more effectively in your relationships. You're more intent in your focus on your hobbies. You're more comfortable spending your time on planning for vacations and enjoying those moments.

TIME ISN'T THE PROBLEM TAKEAWAYS:

1. Thinking about my week, does it offer Level 3 energy? I can juice it up to put me in a state of level 3 by doing this.
2. Do the Wheel of Life exercise at the back of the book. Look at what you consider your strengths and weaknesses.

3. When I look at each of the roles in my life, I can do these things to become more balanced.
4. This has to happen for me to feel successful in each role I identified.

THE SECRET SAUCE FOR LOVE

A man came to me looking for coaching to save his marriage. He was very involved and successful in his career, but his wife was just about ready to serve him with divorce papers. "You're not the man that I married," she'd told him. "You're not the passionate warrior I once knew. Look at your body; you're not doing the things that you're supposed to do to take care of yourself."

The man was surprised to hear this. He'd thought everything was okay between him and his wife. Not great—he realized that much—but not awful, either. As far as he was concerned, he was comfortable in his marriage and had no incentive to change his ways.

Comfort is a state of delusion that blinds us to the lack of growth and development in our lives. In this man's case, he went about his day-to-day business totally unaware of how his marriage was deteriorating slowly over time. Because he thought things were fine, it never occurred to him to consider what was happening in his wife's mind. He didn't do anything deliberately wrong. There was no one single awful event that made his wife unhappy. Her sadness was a gradual unfolding.

The analogy would be like looking at a piece of your hair. On a day-to-day basis, you don't notice that it's growing. It's only when you look over a space of time that you realize how much change has taken place.

My job, as his coach, was to ask him some questions.

- How do you look at your marriage?
- Do you expect the worst or believe in the best of your spouse?
- What is her primary love language?
- How specifically are you meeting her needs?
- How much of the time you spend with your wife is quality time?
- Is change possible?

The man revealed that he spent very little quality time with his wife. He admitted he had taken his wife for granted. Also, when he stopped to really think, he also realized he wasn't getting the support and love from his wife that he craved either.

We took a hard look at the things that he was doing in the relationship. He had a whole list of items he called *have to dos*. These were things his wife expected him to do as part of his role of spouse. He rebelled against the demands, and he didn't feel appreciated. He believed what his wife wanted from him was *heavy and arduous*. In other words, there were times he was expecting the worst.

It's hard to have a happy marriage with those feelings burdening the atmosphere.

One of my favorite books on marriage relationships is Gary Chapman's *The Five Love Languages*. I love his contention that there are five ways that we typically fill up with love. I set out to discover the languages of love that would work for this couple. The most important ones that resonated for them were quality time, words of affirmation, and act of service.

But just knowing that wasn't enough. We had to find a way to put those things into their schedule. It wasn't enough for the husband to tell the wife, "I'll take out the garbage for you when I have the time." He needed to put this activity on his schedule as a regular, ongoing event, and make this as important to him as getting in his car to go to work.

That's not all. Remember the importance of language? In the subject line of his schedule, he created a new role to characterize this task: *Loving Act of Service*. He used this role to describe all of the activities that before this had been on his dreaded "have to-do" list; things like raking the leaves, putting away the dishes, and washing the car. He also color coded this role, choosing the color red to remind him of the passion he had for his wife.

By using this system, this man transformed his marriage in about thirty days. "Man, she is exuberant!" he beamed.

By the way, not only did he improve his relationship with his wife, he reinvigorated his relationship with himself. Because he wanted to show up as her hero, he achieved a strong sense of purpose in his life, which made him feel happier about himself. This inspired him to take care of the areas of his life that were malnourished, which resulted in his addressing his diet and physical fitness. He lost weight, got in great shape, and that made him feel like a better man.

MAKING TIME ON YOUR SCHEDULE

Expectations.

According to many studies that look at the factors that cause divorce, how a spouse is expected to behave is a primary reason behind whether a marriage succeeds of fails. When a spouse expects the worst of their partner, chances are they'll end up in divorce. But those who have very passionate long lasting marriages believe in the best of their partner. Sure, they realize they're going to have some difficulty from time to time, and they may have some disappointments, because that's par for the course in life for everyone. But overall they believe in the core strength of their union, and they reinforce that belief on a periodic basis. They find ways to keep reminding each other why they got married in the first place, and why they truly believe in "till death do us part".

If you desire to spend more time with your spouse, don't keep that thought in your head. Take action! Put that time on your schedule. Use the visual, the auditory and the kinesthetic to empower you to follow through on this commitment. Use the role that inspires you as added reinforcement.

I recommend the all married couples take a close look at what they do for their spouses. Try to find a way to transform the *have to* experiences into acts of service, or whatever you call that term. Find the language that works for you. Find the color that works for you.

Don't limit this practice to regular events. Schedule random times to perform acts of service for your spouse. The specifics will be up to you, depending on what things would be appreciated by your spouse. Then put them into your schedule. Find time for them to pop up.

If you are unsure of what an acceptable act of service would be, ask! Look at things from your spouse's point of view. If you're a man, realize that the term "physical touch" doesn't automatically mean intercourse to a woman. A woman's craving for touch might mean having her husband run his hands through her hair or massage her feet. She might get turned off or even repulsed if her husband bypasses all foreplay to get to the main event. But you'll never know for sure if you don't ask. Seek to clarify rather than make assumptions. Then schedule the time for action.

If you need help on how to be a more attentive spouse, get educated. Most of us today haven't been raised in an environment to know how to be an extraordinary husband or a wife. Is that an excuse or an explanation? If it's an excuse you'll say, "I'm this way and I can't improve because my parents didn't give me the skills." Go ahead and be the victim. Blame somebody else and stay exactly the way you are. Is that what you really want?

Of course not!

If you find yourself in this situation, realize you need to reframe this as an explanation. You're grateful that you've had this wake-up call and are ready to take action. If you need specific guidance, there are tons of books and Internet resources out there. Another book I'd recommend is Elliot Katz's *Being the Strong Man a Woman Wants*. Give yourself thirty minutes every other day to read for self-improvement. Create a role for your subject line. Some possible examples are, *worshipping my spouse* or *bridge to a passionate, exciting future.*

This kind of empowering language emphasizes that this self-education is not homework or a chore, it's the elixir you need to make a successful marriage. Which would you rather have, a chore or an elixir? Not much of a debate here, huh.

To this very day I don't understand why our universities don't offer class credits on how to have an exceptional marriage. We spend years learning information that is unlikely to be used in life and just "wing it" for our relationships. Empower yourself and create your own winning formula through the paths of authors like Gary Chapman, David Deida, Elliot Katz, and Rev. Billy Graham.

Still not sure what your actual next step should be? Let's go back to the movie theater. What do you want the movie with you and your spouse, as co-star, to look like? Is this an epic adventure? A lighthearted romantic comedy? A deeply passionate romance? A XXX double feature?

Whichever one you choose, your story will be a blockbuster success as long as you put the time in your schedule and remember those magic words: persistence and commitment. If it's an adventure you want, schedule out twenty minutes to brainstorm on how to have that adventure. Maybe it's going on a hike somewhere unique. Maybe it's inviting your spouse to go sailing. If it's romance, maybe you'll ask yourself, "Where can we just go on a quick weekend jaunt and get away on a surprise little mini vacation?"

Figure out the purpose of the experience. What do you want to create?

In my role as *Radiance Worshipper*, I want to make sure that my wife is happy and stress free. I've already explained how I use language to help motivate me to perform loving acts of service for her. Together we've also created rules that help ensure we don't start to take each other for granted. For example, no phone calls or texting when we're riding in the car together. Our time is to be shared and our intent is not to let distractions pull our attention away.

My wife works and loves what she does, but at one point I saw her getting a little testy because she had a lot on her plate. Her stress level was on the verge of causing a strain in our relationship.

I decided I needed to take action. I called up her employer and asked, "When can I schedule a surprise, four-day weekend to send her away?"

They gave me the dates. I sent her down to the Caribbean for four days, by herself, and told her to have fun. Then I called up the hotel and said, "Make sure she has an incredible experience." That was a gift of service that would never have happened if I had not taken the time to create a special experience for her.

Am I genius? No. Am I a magical guru with a special love potion? No. All I am is a man who loves his wife and made a commitment to show that love by taking an action. It's not rocket science, really. All it takes is takes is desire and —here's that word again — planning.

Here are the specifics of how I made it happen. In my calendar, I scheduled twenty minutes under *Radiance Worshipper*. In the body of the calendar I added the note, "Let me make a 10-minute phone call to the employer." At the time, I didn't have an exact plan on what I was going to do; I just knew that I was going to do something.

Then the next day I put thirty minutes in my schedule to investigate where I could send her on short notice that wasn't going to kill our finances. I knew the trip had to happen quickly, and airlines love to take advantage of those last minute bookings.

However, thirty minutes ended up not being enough time. After searching through tons of websites I hadn't found a solution that worked. I ended up doing what I should have done in the first place. I made a two-minute call to a travel agent I knew, and let her do all the work. In the end I was able to create an incredible experience for my spouse, using a little resourcefulness and thirty-two minutes.

I should add here that I learned all this the hard way. My current wife is my *second* wife.

My first attempt at marriage lasted for ten years, and for most of that time we struggled. We probably never should have gotten married in the first place, but I was young and foolish and didn't have the courage to call it quits before we got married. What I realized along the way is that you can love somebody but maybe not still be in love with them. There was a lot of heartache, a lot of soul-searching and, in the end, a lot of heartbreak.

She deserved somebody who could give her what she needed. Unfortunately, that wasn't me. The marriage ended ugly. The last time I ever spoke to her she said I'd wasted ten years of her life.

I was dumbfounded by her response. I didn't see things the way she did. I'd come out of the experience realizing that I deserved to get what I wanted, instead of accepting what I got. I chose to see that I'm a more caring person because of those ten years, because of that pain and because of the heartache I went through.

I could have used that marriage as an excuse to never get involved in a relationship again by reveling in the role of victim and using that crutch to prevent myself from loving again.

I chose instead to look at my experience as an explanation. I transformed the heartache into an opportunity to get things right. I realized I had the opportunity for a second take.

I told myself that if I was going to have another marriage, good would not be good enough. Good to me would be a poor marriage, something okay but just not memorable. I didn't want to cause heartache for another woman, as I had with my first wife. I needed to prove that I could be a husband who was worthy of a woman's love.

But I also needed to believe the best in me, that I could change. My role was not to change this person; I needed to change. I need to improve myself for me, first, and then as a result be able to give everything to my wife. I worked on myself, and when I was ready to look for another life partner, I decided this would be somebody whom I could embrace and support when she was at her ugliest. If I could love her at her worst, I could support her even more at her best.

For a woman like that, a trip to the Caribbean was the least I could do.

TIME ISN'T THE PROBLEM TAKEAWAYS:

1. These are five ways that I can honor my spouse or partner.
2. Look, the time I spend with my significant other isn't cutting it anymore. These are the things I will change to improve the situation.

YOU ARE WHO YOU DECIDE TO BE

"No one is ever defeated until defeat has been accepted as reality"
—Napoleon Hill

Most studies of nature versus nurture consider our genes as nature, and our external environment, particularly our childhood upbringing, as environment. While genes and outside environment may be enough to explain the characteristics and behavior of fruit flies, it is not enough to explain the characteristics and behaviors of man. They do not determine who we are and how we behave.

Humans have free will. As Tony Robbins says, "It's not our conditions, but our decisions that shape our future." We direct our own environment to a greater degree than do other living things. We choose our focus and we make decisions that affect the trajectory of our lives.

Don't believe me? Well, one famous study focused on identical twin brothers who had an alcoholic father. The goal was to learn about the influence of genes on our characteristics. One of the twins was an alcoholic, homeless bum on the street, and the other was a very wealthy, very successful tycoon in the business world. The scientists interviewed them both, hoping for insight as to why they ended up so different, despite their identical genes and their presumably similar environments.

The alcoholic son told them, "Well, I grew up with an alcoholic father. Alcohol was in the house all the time. I saw my dad drinking. So I guess it was natural enough that I became an alcoholic, too".

The son who was not an alcoholic said, "Well, I grew up with an alcoholic father. Alcohol was in the house all the time. I saw my dad drinking, and I saw what it did to him and to my family. So I guess it was natural enough that I swore I would never be like that, and so I don't drink!"

Exact same environment yet two different outcomes. One used alcoholism as an excuse. The other used this disease as an explanation.

I mention this story of the brothers here to make this point: We choose who we are. Not our parents. Not society. Not some unseen force in the universe. It's up to us to decide where we go in our lives. If we're dissatisfied with the direction, we're the ones who can make the course correction.

But making the decision to change can be clumsy and awkward. Setting out into the unknown always is, just like in the earlier example of learning how to drive a car. The first time you come face to face with a stick shift, you might say, "I didn't even know there was such a thing as manual versus automatic." But when you realize you need to learn, you become what we call consciously incompetent. "Oh, I didn't know I needed to know how to do this."

You may initially be really excited about learning this new skillset but have a very low competence; you've begun at the enthusiastic beginner stage. If you just start on one piece and get skilled at that, then you move to what is called conscious competence. You practice the steps, and if you keep going through that pattern then you'll become an expert.

By doing that you will meet and reach unconscious competence; High competence, high commitment peak performer. This just becomes the way that you think. You no longer have to rely on writing everything down, as it just becomes part of what's in your head. You get empowering abilities.

The same holds true for any changes you make in your life path. Changing the trajectory of your life isn't automatic. This involves adopting new habits, new behaviors and new ways of thinking. This is going to be awkward. Doing something new and unfamiliar always is. The problem for most of us is the stage between enthusiastic beginner and peak performer. There is a point where you may want to quit; the disillusioned learner. That is when both competence and commitment is low. Commitment becomes low primarily because you come across unforeseen problems in your quest for learning something new and you don't get answers.

This is where others quit. In the past, you too, might have tried something new and have quit at this point. But not now. Not anymore. Now you have the knowledge to realize that, because you have enough strength in the purpose itself, you will move into capable but cautious performer. Your competence will be fairly high and commitment will regain its strength.

TRAJECTORY OF CHANGE			
STAGE	COMMITMENT LEVEL	CONFIDENCE LEVEL	COMPETENCE LEVEL
Beginner	High	Low	Low
Disillusioned Intermediate	Low	Low	Low—Gives Up
Intermediate Who Doesn't Give up	High	Growing	Consciously Competent
Pro	High	High	Unconsciously Competent

Additionally, you are not starting from scratch in this process. All you are doing is building on the foundation of what you already know. This isn't only about just adding a bunch of new stuff to your tool box. This is about taking what you're already doing and becoming masterful in that before you add the others. This is not unlike the process used by a black belt master, who keeps working and working at what he already knows, and in the process achieves mastery through practice.

Look at where you have been successful in the other areas of your life. Then take those successes and immerse yourself with these tools. Tell yourself, "I'm just going to start with this one, and when I have that mastered then I'll choose whether I want to go on the next one or not."

Then when you take on the next step, you're faced with another opportunity/challenge. Can I do it? What happens if I stumble here? What if I conclude this is all too much trouble to bother?

Remember, you are not alone. If you've planned right, you've got a friend or mentor or coach to help, and they will pick you up and keep moving you forward. They will give you the fruit and the food to nourish, rebuild and regain that strength so that you can go and cross the finish line.

As a coach, I often look at myself as the guy on the edge of the mud pit looking down and holding the tree branch or holding the rope. I tell my client to hang on tight and be willing to do the work to pull yourself out, because if I do it for you, you will climb back down in the hole eventually. But as a coach know that I will never let go of that rope or branch, and I'll be waiting for when you are ready to begin.

- *Create a list of accomplishments you had to earn and were meaningful.*
- *Did you celebrate your victories?*
- *If not, how can you celebrate them right now?*
- *How can you use those tools, skills, and lessons for one challenge in your life right now?*
- *What are five changes or actions that you can take in the next 30 days that will move you forward?*

WORKING WITH THE UNIVERSE

The Universe rewards unequally in some situations. Sometimes The Universe does not reward you in the same effort that you give, and careers don't either. If somebody receives an unexpected windfall, that's great. Blessings like that happen sometimes when we least expect them. However, we would be wise NOT to expect life to unfairly reward us.

I've seen this in my own life. Remember how I said I joined The Marines? Admittedly, I went in as a bit of a mama's boy, and they did a fine job in turning me into a man. In the process, however, they also left me with some self-limiting beliefs, mostly by making me feel hyper-masculine and loathe to express my emotions. While this thinking may work for The Marines, I ran into trouble when transferring that way of being into a relationship. This was partially why my first marriage collapsed.

Leaving The Marines also left me with my first identity crisis. Who was I? How did the skills I learned as a soldier relate to civilian life? Do I change my standards?

I had a very long journey to go through to be able to look in the mirror and say, "Yes, you can be the great qualities of the Marine and also be more, and be able to use that leverage to be something else." Then as soon as I felt good about myself again and achieved success in the corporate world, I was feeling undone by my boss, whom I felt was acting irrationally and asking the impossible of me.

Now I'll take responsibility and say that at the time I didn't have the tools and skill set to communicate effectively with this boss. Perhaps if I had known of a way to make that a win/win situation, I might still be at that corporate job today.

However, what seemed like a bad situation at the time turned into a blessing in disguise. My frustration about those working conditions and desire to get out of the ninety-hour work week spurred me toward my dream of retirement. I used those emotions as the baton to keep me moving forward, to keep my head held high as I did my planning to escape that world.

Underneath, though, was a person in shambles saying, "I can't hack it in the corporate world anymore. What am I going to do now?" I was also worried about how I was looking to others. Would my family consider me a failure? Ultimately, if I couldn't make a go of it, who was I?

If those were the only thoughts in my head, I would have been doomed. However, by keeping my focus on my goal and being persistent, I kept telling myself, "As long as I don't give up I can't lose. As long as I just throw one more pebble, take one more step, I will keep moving closer to that finish line and cross it to victory."

I'd be lying if I said it wasn't painful or didn't take work. True transformation happens when you're willing to get outside of your comfort zone and then take one step beyond that and then another. The reality is that you need to build habits. Habits are made through persistence, through creating and doing the things you desire over and over again.

You can do it in a way that still brings a smile to your face and some sweat to your brow. It's possible to do both.

Here are some simple truths.

- Decide who you want to be.
- Choose your goals and then work conscientiously at achieving them.
- More often than not, The Universe will reward you for your work, and you will get back from life what you put in.

TIME ISN'T THE PROBLEM TAKEAWAYS:

1. These are the things that keep me up at night.
2. Here's my biggest goal. The obstacles I see preventing me from reaching it are? This is what I'm doing to make them self-imposed limitations.

LIFE IS UNFAIR—GET OVER IT

Sometimes when life hands you a rotten egg, you've got to force yourself to smile.

There's a great scene in the movie *Rocky Balboa (aka Rocky VI)* that I absolutely love and find incredibly inspiring. Rocky's talking to his son who sees himself as a victim and feels he's always been in the shadow of Rocky's success.

Rocky says to him, "Life can be cruel. It is a mean and cruel world that will knock you down and beat you to the ground and not want you to get back up."

Truer words have never been spoken. Yes, life can be unfair. Events will occur that keep holding you down, so you might as well get used to it. "But it's not about how many times you get hit, it's how many times you get hit and keep moving forward, how many times you get hit and keep getting up. That is how winning is done."

If you know what you're worth, go out and get what your worth. But don't keep blaming him or her or somebody else for you not doing what you know you've been brought into this world to do. You have a gift. Don't rob the world of that incredible gift, that passion that's inside of you, because somebody you love has told you to settle, or said that you shouldn't get too far ahead of yourself. That person is, in effect, hitting you and knocking you down.

Too often you choose not to see your situation that way. You look at the person whom you know loves and cares about you. You believe that what they have to say must have merit and must be given attention.

The only problem is—and this can be a tragic one at times—they don't recognize that they're knocking you down every day. They believe they're giving you sage advice in your own best interests. Whether it's your co-worker, your boss, or your loved one. They all have great intentions...but sometimes they have poor judgment.

You have to be wise and reject that judgment. You have to have the willpower to say, "I'm going to keep moving forward. I'm going to keep getting up." There's a flame burning inside you, dying to be expressed, and you're not going to let anyone's misguided words of advice stop you.

You need to be courageous to step out beyond your comfort zone. But my hope is that you can share what you want with the world and are able to radiate that out and create the energy that is abundantly inside of you.

I'd like you to say right now, out loud, "World, this is who I am. This is what I have to offer, and I'm not going to hide anymore."

When I watch clients of mine make this declaration, its power sometimes startles the crap out of me and raises the hair on my arms. The energy of those words is unbelievable.

When you've accepted the challenge, when you've said, "I'm going to cross over. I must." It's not *I want to*, not *I should*, it's *I must*. There is no other route. Burn the boats because there is no other way off this island but to conquer all challenges.

BEWARE THE NAYSAYERS... ESPECIALLY THE BIGGEST ONE OF ALL

Your best friends can be your worst enemies on your road to success.

One of the hardest obstacles to face might come from those well-meaning folks who are supposed to be there to support you, but who try to discourage you with words like, "I'm telling you this because I care and I don't want to see you fail. I don't want to see you hurt". Or, "This is great, this might be your hobby, but we can't afford this now."

I was able to see that my family, who loved me and wanted the best for me, was really holding me back. They were constantly sending me the message, "Don't set your bar too high."

Keep in mind, these family members didn't realize they were doing this. In fact, if I challenged them directly they would have vehemently denied they were doing anything but wanting the best for me. However, the words they used and the actions they took were telling me to live small, not large.

Fortunately, I was able to realize they were talking about their bar. Not mine. I believed I had innate gifts to share and that those gifts had nothing to do with them.

Yes, those pesky naysayers can hold you back. But don't be fooled. The biggest naysayer of all is going to be the person facing you in the mirror.

That's right. You. Your little voice in your head thinks thousands of times before anything ever comes out of your mouth. Much of what's there isn't pretty, lots of self-limiting beliefs that serve to keep you stuck in your tracks. That's why you find those so-called words of wisdom from your friends warning you to watch out very comforting. They're the same words, thoughts, and ideas you're already telling yourself.

They're also the very words you should be ignoring!

When you think and do an action over and over it becomes a habit. Over the years, you've most likely built some really strong habits that have told you to do what you do because society says this or that, or don't do that because you'll stand out. They may make you feel better, but they won't lead to your success.

BE YOUR OWN CHEERLEADER

> *"We can fail doing what we don't love, so you might as well take a chance doing what you love"*
>
> **—Jim Carrey**

I would personally rather be somebody who stands out as unusual because of my successes—or because at least I tried—than to never have tried at all or at least gone on that journey. I want to encourage you to do the same, but at the same time, I have to be honest. You're going to stumble on your way to success, and that's where the resources in this book will come in handy.

During your difficult times, as your coach, I'll simply tell you this isn't a one or two-day or a two-week process. Yes, it's that irksome word "time" again, and the only problem here is how you take advantage of it. In order to change over to a new way of thinking, you'll have to wean yourself away from processes and habits that you've embraced for a long time, perhaps even for decades. To do this, you're going to need a minimum of thirty days to create this new habit and absorb it into your being.

You're also going to need a valid measurement for your progress. As an example of what I mean here, let's go back to our stalwart example of exercise. If you're working out, you typically need forty-five days before you start seeing results. You might get discouraged, however, if you're judging your progress solely on the amount of weight you're losing. That's because when you first start working out muscle weighs more than fat. But if you measure with a body fat content scale, you would see that you're dropping the fat, which is your real goal, and get a real sense of success.

The same thing is the case here; you're going to stumble (remember the disillusioned learner) if you're not using the right navigation, the right tools, the right beacon, to show you you're still on track, that you're still heading in the right direction.

DON'T FORGET YOUR POSSE

> *"Keep away from people who try to belittle your ambitions. Small people always do that, but the really great ones make you feel that you, too, can become great."*
>
> —**Mark Twain**

Several generations ago, the idea of having to tell someone to surround themselves with people who share their goals might have seemed like an oxymoron. People were naturally more connected back then. Today, our world is changing regardless of whether you are in your twenties or AARP years, and many people are choosing to live alone.

Eric Klinenberg, who wrote *Going Solo: The Extraordinary Rise and Surprising Appeal of Living Alone,* found in his research that in 1950, twenty-two percent of American adults were single, four million of them lived alone, and they made up a paltry nine percent of households. Today, by contrast, more than fifty percent of American adults are single, thirty-one million of them live alone, and they make up a hefty twenty-eight percent of households.

If you live alone, you might believe you can handle anything by yourself. Yes, you can be your own cheerleader. But you'll have even greater success by surrounding yourself with people who will really support you.

Warning: Remember, these people may not be the ones who are closest to you.

While your loved ones want the best for you, they often make lousy cheerleaders. That's because when close family members and friends see you making changes—positive changes—in your life, you might set off their fear radar. Their own insecurities may make them fear that you'll change so much you'll want to leave them. They might even do things to unknowingly sabotage you in order to keep you in their lives.

That's a trap you'll want to avoid. You don't want to be sucked back into the same old habits that were killing you, not allowing you to be passionate, not allowing you to live life and preventing you from going where you want. The way that you can do that is to immerse yourself among people who support the ideals and support the outcomes that you want. If you want to improve your fitness, go join a running club, go join a biking club, or join a walking group.

Call up a friend and say, "Would you like to go hiking? Would you like to go walking?" Sign up for a race. Do something that holds you accountable instead of just keeping your thoughts to yourself. Do something to have other people say, "You said you're going to do this, how can I really support you and help you? Are you going to walk the walk or are you just going to talk the talk because we want to support you on that? By the way, we'll be there at the finish line, ready to hold you, raise you up and celebrate with you."

But once you do that, those challenges are going to be there. That's why you need to add celebration time to your schedule and to your appointments. How often? Constantly.

Go out and notice the small victories of the day, things like doing one extra rep, playing one extra round, skipping the ice cream and eating the salad. Those are the things you'll want to celebrate constantly, as these little things eventually start to add up.

As an example, I was just working with a client whose son was invited to go to Yale for crew, the boat racing team. He has another son who isn't as successful, and he's really challenged because this son is taking on all this man's undesirable characteristics.

There's the old adage, "do as I say, not as I do". One son did as the father said, and the other one did not. He asked me how to change that.

I offered that he had to lead by example, and as a first step he needed to celebrate. "You concentrate on focusing on the small victories and minimize the focus on what's not right. If you're looking for where there are moments of celebration, that's what you'll see. That's what you should seek out and celebrate."

"Do not let what you cannot do interfere with what you can do."
—John Wooden

I used his son going to Yale as an example. I told him that most of us would make up rules around this event that would go something like this: "Yes, I'm happy you got accepted into Yale and were a star at crewing in high school, but we're not at a point where we should really be celebrating that yet. Let's see how you do in college." Then after the son gets to Yale, thrives and gets a degree, you then might say, "Until you put that degree to use I'm really not going to celebrate because you haven't proven that you really have the ability to apply what you learned." Then once he gets a job you might say, "Until you earn loads of money we're really not going to celebrate."

My client could have chosen to operate under those rules. If he did, he would have missed out on celebrating all those little victories that happened along the way: the acceptance into a tough school, the success achieved in that competitive environment, each race event, each semester of grades, the degree that was earned, and the nice job that was the result of all that hard work.

My point is to celebrate the victories along the way because those are far more numerous than the short-lived big victories. When you do that you also enjoy the journey along the way and gain the motivation to keep going. It's akin to running a marathon. You're more likely to stay on the path if you celebrate the completion of every mile, than if you wait until you cross the finish line.

PERSISTENCE AND DISCIPLINE

I can appreciate that we need to be incredibly careful with the words that we use when we're tired, when we're worn out, with our children. We let things slip, and we don't necessarily mean them, but they just come out. Just imagine if you walked into your child's room and found crayon scribbles all over the wall. Your first reaction might be to yell at your child and punish him or her harshly. Later on, you might regret any overreaction, understanding in the calmness of reflection that he or she was acting out of creative self-expression and hadn't been taught limits. But the damage was already done. The punishment in all likelihood would have a lasting effect on the child.

If there's any comfort in this, it's in the knowledge that you're not alone. Everyone, even if they're not a parent, has done something they've come to later regret. It comes with the territory of being a human.

Count me in as part of the human race. I've acted carelessly as a parent, as well, and have done lots of things that I've later regretted. Perhaps my own behavior was one of the reasons I was drawn to psychology. Learning all about how the human mind works, helped me realize that evolving my psychology was essential if I were to lead the life I truly wanted.

How did I evolve? Two factors were critical. I've mentioned them before but they bear repeating again now. Persistence and discipline.

Let me shout that out from the proverbial rooftop: **PERSISTENCE AND DISCIPLINE!**

Now, why do persistence and discipline matter? I'm not asking you to go across the Grand Canyon or climb Mount Everest. However, consider that even a drop of water, over time, erodes a piece of granite. If you have discipline and persistently stay on the path you create for yourself—a path that is defined by your purpose—you will continually build up what really matters in your life.

There's an important distinction to be made here. Discipline and persistence are musts, yes, but if they're not tied to your purpose you may make it down the track but you won't cross the finish line. That's because discipline and persistence without purpose makes you susceptible to temptation, and it's very easy to let yourself get distracted when you don't have the counterbalancing force of purpose to keep you focused on your goal.

Do you want to know what human kryptonite is? It's limp language and words. Words are enough alone to keep us from taking actions. Words alone are enough to keep us stagnant. We have a choice. If you haven't read Viktor Frankl's, *Man's Search for Meaning,* I highly recommend that you do, because at the end, he reminds us that it's all about choice. As Frankl points out, a person can endure the greatest of hardships, up until the freedom of choice is taken away. Once a person chooses to relinquish the freedom of choice, he or she loses the will to choose to live.

No one can make you do anything without first getting your consent. You can be in prison but nobody can imprison your mind. Ask Nelson Mandela who was imprisoned for over twenty-seven years. When they interviewed him upon his release, they asked, "How did you endure being in there?"

He said "I didn't endure. I prepared."

Language and meaning starts in our mind. Let's go back to those self-limiting thoughts in your head? What if those thoughts were positive and empowering and not deprecating and restrictive? As Gandhi says, "There's a process there and what you think becomes."

In essence, what you think becomes your habits and your habits become your values, and your values are what you live out. Are you picking up kryptonite when you speak? Are you using limp language that prevents you from taking actions? Think about this. Your identity is created and supported by the various roles you will execute in your day, your week, your life.

What if there was a "make it go button" that you could push to bring all your roles in order to turn all the responsibilities you have in life into incredible experiences? What if you could make your hopes and dreams really come into focus? What are the pictures and videos you would share with your friends and family as proof of how exciting your life is?

BELIEVING IN NO LIMITS

Be forewarned, a high quality life takes planning, discipline and strength. If you can learn to master the skills needed, they will bring big payoff to you personally.

There are four types of ways that you can do this:

1. Doing it — Implementing the steps needed to achieve your goal.
2. Delete it/Not do it — Decide that something is not beneficial and move on.
3. Leverage it - Delegate by making the outcome someone else's responsibility.
4. Defer it — Put off the decision for another time.

I will talk a little later about the Do It Now, Not Doing Now, and Not Doing Never skills, and how you can use them to really make an impact in your life.

Life is a roller coaster. Life is about ebb and flow, and there's times it's going to be tough. There's times where it's going to knock you down and you're not going to want to get up.

If you're in the position where times are difficult, ask yourself if you're looking at your situation as an excuse or an explanation? Are you allowing events to happen to you, are you using them as a crutch to hold yourself in place? Are you being deliberate to defer something or using it to procrastinate?

Yes, you may be in a position where finances are difficult, you're struggling in your marriage, or you're trying to get in shape. You'd rather want to find more time to spend on your hobbies, improve your relationships, have more time with your kids, or get the body you've always dreamed of having.

When you're in a tough situation, it's easy to see yourself as the victim. The question is, are you a victim or the effect of other people's behaviors and decisions? Are you the effect of the environment? The answer to that is up to you. The reality is that you can be the cause. The world is going to change, and change is inevitable. Growth is optional. That moment of decision is when you have to decide: Do I want to be the cause? Do I want to be the reason why I catapult forward?

The important thing to remember is that you have a choice. My recommendation is to get a coach, surround yourself with friends, or use any available resources that will support you. Then, become resourceful yourself. Don't believe you have zero choices or that your choices are limited to black or white.

In other words, keep your options open. Make a list what options are available even if they're the most far-fetched options out there.

Don't justify or defend before you've even gotten them out. Don't think logically or mentally. Think from the heart, from what you truly desire and believe.

For example, if you want to be more involved in your grown children's lives and be more of a grandparent, what are your options? You could fly to them. You could fly them to you. You could schedule more vacation time with them. You might communicate more over the Internet.

Right there alone, are at least four options. But often what prevents us from taking action is believing in the lack of either time or money. Those are limiting beliefs. The reality is there are always solutions. Once you get that third, fourth, fifth, sixth item out, then you can go back and work through the merits, the pros and cons of each, which one has the best probability for the outcome that you want, and narrow down your options.

Here is where you should connect with yourself and ask yourself a series of questions. If you consider yourself "brave", try this in front of a mirror.

- Is now the right time or do I have to wait for conditions to change?
- Which way do I go?
- What am I made of?
- What am I being called to do?
- Am I letting society make the decision for me?
- Do I believe I'm unworthy?
- Do I believe I'm not entitled to go forward?
- How do I believe in myself?
- Where do I have the persistence to follow my plan?
- Where will I be three months from now if don't take this action?
- What will my life be like if don't do this?

- How can I turn any of these answers that have limitations into execution?

I think many people look themselves in the mirror and have regrets about not giving their all. I know that I would rather try and fail than to not try at all, because to me failing is only when I haven't even tried. I could live with trying and failing. I could not live with giving up when the possibility of success was still out there.

> *"A coward dies a thousand times before his death, but the valiant taste of death but once."*
>
> **—William Shakespeare**

HOW TO QUIET THAT CHATTERBOX IN YOUR HEAD

Sometimes, this means telling your mind to "Shut Up!"

Just like that baseball player who developed roles to counteract the negative thoughts his mind was telling him, you'll need to come up with your own way of neutralizing that ugly voice in your head. There are a lot of techniques out there: daily affirmations, hypnotherapy, Para liminal tapes, yoga, and group therapy, just to name a few. You may have to experiment until you come up with the practice or practices that resonate best with you.

It took me some time to find the right formula, but I've found success through meditation techniques, yoga, endurance racing, and solitary nature walks. When you shut off your mind like this, you're able to really connect with your soul and with who you truly are. Doing this can help you discover the answers to the questions you need to ask yourself. This can give you the courage to change a *should do someday* into a *must do now.*

TIME ISN'T THE PROBLEM TAKEAWAYS:

1. This is one area of my life where I'm holding myself back.
2. These are the things preventing me from taking action and having a breakthrough in my life.
3. These are the four ways I will change the outcome.
4. This has to happen for me to change my schedule this week and the four items actually occur.

THIS ONE THING CAN MAKE ALL THE DIFFERENCE

I've already talked about the importance of having a brotherhood or a community where you can be around like-minded people. It's not just important, it's *critical* to insuring your success.

How do you do this? One way to look at assembling your group is to imagine you're the king of a kingdom.

- Who are the trusted advisors at your roundtable?
- What characteristics make them trustworthy and worthy of your respect?
- Who are the ones who will look out for your best interests and are strong enough to offer you the advice you *need* to hear.

Choose them wisely. Seek out people who may have skills and talents you lack, who can shore up your gaps. I believe that we'll never be great at the things we're weak at. Don't try to be. I mean the President of the United States isn't perfect. It's why he has a cabinet, and he relies on those people as his advisors. All presidents do this. The advisors keep him on track and are there to offer guidance and support when needed.

If you look around your life, you'll find people whom you would be honored to have on your own advisory council. A loving spouse, adult child, trusted sibling, faithful friend, for example. You might even extend your circle wider to include people such as a religious advisor, paid coach, or business mentor.

I have been fortune to have such a community of advisors in my life. Because I have taken this action, I now have people around me who can shore up my weaknesses and respect and support my vision.

I find my community very useful when I decide to take on something new, like pick up a new hobby or learn a new language. Teaching an old dog like me new tricks isn't easy (as any adult who tries to learn a new language finds out), but when my community "has my back", I have a giant support system behind me and my goals.

When I decide to tackle a new project, I tell people, "I'm going to do this". Now that doesn't mean I necessarily have a plan in place. But this public declaration holds me accountable. I'm not inclined to let myself off the hook when the going gets rough. My advisors are there to tell me to tow that line, and they will support me in doing that. But mostly having them around helps ensure I don't fail for the simple reason that I don't want egg on my face. If I make a public pronouncement of my goal, I'm much more likely to follow through.

By the way, before I do commit to making a public announcement, I determine its importance and if I'm truly willing to stand behind it. This serves as another way of clarifying my wants and needs.

As I've said before, change is not easy, and having a support system behind you makes all the difference. For example, when I ran my first marathon, I hit the proverbial wall. I was at about mile nineteen out of 26.2, and I still had some ways to go. I wanted to quit. However, I had prepared for this possibility by making sure others knew I was running this race. I was able to tell myself, "There are people waiting for me at the finish line, and if I don't show up, this will be a failure I'm going to have to live with for the rest of my life."

With that, I was able to keep going one more step forward. Then another. I didn't care that I was reduced to walking, or that I'd end up with a terrible time, and my legs were killing me. I was determined to keep going, because I didn't want to live with the idea of quitting. I didn't want to have to go back home, look myself in that mirror, and admit I hadn't been willing to give it my best shot.

You know what? Somehow I got my second wind and finished strong. Life often works that way. You hit a rough patch and want to give up right there. But if you hang in there, you just might get the payoff others only dream of achieving.

TIME ISN'T THE PROBLEM TAKEAWAYS:

1. These are my knights of the roundtable. I choose them because…
2. This is a goal I would like to achieve. I would pick this advisor to hold me accountable.

LIVING A LIFE YOU LOVE

The coaching director of the Tony Robbins Organization, the Robbins Research International, once asked me, "Chad, you have a unique view on how you do vacations. How do you fit them into your work?"

I said, "Marc, you got it backwards. Work fits in between my vacations."

When you lead from your values then you'll find room for the other responsibilities in your life. Resourcefulness opens up for you. It's a way of giving purpose to your personal time.

IT'S OKAY TO HAVE FUN

As I have mentioned earlier, one of my main reasons for retiring was to be able to have time to devote to my son. I wanted him to learn from my character—both the positive and the imperfect parts.

One way we're able to do this is by taking road trips. A few years ago, as an example, we drove to the very tip of the Upper Peninsula of

Michigan, to a place called Isle Royale. Isle Royale is populated with about 900 moose and quite a number of wolves, and is the home of the oldest, large prey animal study in the history of the world. It's a very rugged and difficult terrain. In short, the perfect place for some father and son time.

We went on a five-day hike in the wilderness on this island, which was followed by a three-hour boat ride on Lake Superior. That was a treacherous trip, as we had to grapple with monstrously high waves that could have easily sunk a freighter. My son loved every minute. Those are the kinds of memories that leave a lasting impact.

Not only had I wanted to do this, I made it happen.

In the next section, I'll be going into greater detail on how you can achieve a life that matters by planning and executing major events in your life. These include things that right now, in your heart of hearts, you believe you will never get to do. By using these strategies, I now seek out new opportunities and adventures. Then I make time for them, whether they're travel and personal pursuits, devotion, learning experiences, or community service. You name it, my life is fun.

Once you have this gift for creating special moments, share them with other people. Planning effectively will enable you to create more opportunities for fulfillment in your life, and ironically enough, the more you do, the more you will want to do. The trick that took me longer than I'd like to admit is that when I stopped believing that there's not enough to go around, I got filled up in that process more than I could have ever imagined.

GETTING BACK MORE THAN YOU GIVE

One study of 50-65 year olds concluded that forty-nine percent of them did not give anything outside of themselves to anyone else. I believe this is because these particular people are living a life of survival, and don't believe they have enough for themselves let alone anyone else.

However, once you believe you have more than enough—when you're in that state of stability—it's easy to believe you have abundance. Sometimes you get back even more than what you expected.

There was a study done at the Georgia Mental Health Institute in which doctors observed the problems patients were having getting healed. They saw patients upset and hurt, demanding that people love them, and distraught because that love was not forthcoming.

But when these patients learned to give love first, they discovered they did receive the love that they were desperately seeking for themselves. The trick was that they had to give their love away to others to get fulfillment for themselves.

If you truly want to have fulfillment, if you want to have long-lasting passion, satisfaction and happiness in your life, you need to make growth and contribution to others a part of your life.

When you contribute to others, when you take these gifts and you start sharing with your family, your friends, your co-workers, your gardening group, your spouse, your extended family, what you discover is that they have been desperately looking for this oasis themselves. When you get to the oasis you realize there's more than enough water for the entire community to drink, because the spring doesn't cease flowing.

THE PERILS OF DRIFTING

Napoleon Hill wrote about the concept of drifting. He defines drifting as being controlled and influenced by others. I'd say about ninety-seven percent of the world lives in drifting, living a life where you're the effect, not the cause. No wonder so many people find themselves living way off course. Drifting is what prevents us from living a passionate, fulfilling life.

It's important that you understand and recognize when you're drifting, because then you have the ability to get back on course.

Look at where you are in your life. Are you drifting or are you catching that wind in your sails to the best of your ability, making that course correction, and using that momentum to swiftly get to your destination? If drifting is playing a role in your life, how long have you been allowing people to influence where you are? How do you show up each day?

It doesn't take a whole lot of work to go with the flow. Even a dead fish can float downstream. But it does take work to go against the current. You have to have the strength, the conditioning and the endurance to be able to withstand the obstacles life puts in front of you.

If you're working out, do you build muscle by exercising the same way over and over, with the same number of reps that you've always done? Of course you don't. You don't build muscle until you go beyond that resistance point. You need resistance in order to grow the muscle, in order to stretch those fibers and build strength.

The key is knowing when to push and when not to push. Going from lifting twenty-five pound weights up to 100 pounds could really cause some problems. The ensuing frustration could make you give up. However, if you add, say, two and a half pounds instead, that gives you just a little bit of discomfort and is enough to cause your muscles to grow. By adding a little bit at a time, you keep up your commitment and your confidence. Eventually you get to the point of lifting those 100 pounds, and your goal is reached.

TIME ISN'T THE PROBLEM TAKEAWAYS:

1. These are the areas where I have been living in The Effect of other people's decisions.
2. This is what I can do to turn that around and begin living so that I'm The Cause of my own present and future moments.
3. Here are three specific actions —using my juicy language—that will define my character as being in The Cause.

THIS IS THE CHAPTER YOU'RE AFRAID TO READ

"There are two mistakes one can make along the road to truth...not going all the way, and not starting."

—**Buddha**

Are you one of those stubborn ones? Are you insisting on continuing to go down the path that you've always been on? Have you gotten to this part of the book believing, "Aw, he's not talking about me? I'm not the one with the problem."

Sorry, friend. If your life isn't working "right", what makes you think that using the same old tools from your rusty toolbox –you probably don't have a ton of them anyway– are going to get you to a more desirable destination? I honor you for using the tools in first place; however, is it possible that the tools that got you to this point in life may be the exact same things preventing you from getting to the next level you desire?

Take a hard look at what is going on in your life. Do you show up to do plumbing with electrical tools? If you show up with the wrong tools and expect them to work, you might get the job done, but it's going to take a very long time and not be pretty.

Did life hand you a raw deal when you were young? Maybe you need to do something different to create a more positive ending. You don't like the movie script? Change scenes, change locations. Change the script; rewrite the script of your life with the ending you want.

Is it too late to change? The answer is up to you. There's obviously a gap—something that's holding you back at this point. There's a difference between your talents, the skills you've learned, and your unique DNA or the gifts that you were born with. Unless you're six feet under—and I don't see that happening otherwise we wouldn't be having this conversation at this point—it's *never too late* to change your direction. As Mark Twain once said "The two greatest days in life are the day you are born, and the day you discover why."

A great place to start is to ponder the following questions:

- What is it costing me to stay where I'm at right now?
- Why am I here in the first place?
- What's getting in my way?
- What's preventing me from giving my gifts to the world?
- Why do I keep telling myself I feel too tired to take action?
- Why do I keep telling myself I don't have the time to take action?
- Why am I afraid to start?

The answer to any of these questions starts by your realizing that these feelings are stories that you've told and retold yourself about yourself. These are stories you've rehearsed for years, and you've gotten really adept at repeating them.

What's interesting about these stories and why they're very seductive is because there's some actual facts in them, and you're buying those stories, or at least you're pretending and trying to buy them. But the reality is it's simply the way you are acting out.

Therefore, we need to look at how you are behaving. How are you holding yourself physically? Are you slumped and not breathing? Is your head down like a sad or tired person, or do you walk around like you just won the gold medal in the Olympics?

What about your thoughts? Are your thoughts empowering or really defeating questions? Here are a few possibilities that may be rolling around in your head.

- Why don't I have the resources or the money?
- Why do I have a boss who won't give me *fill in the blank*?
- Why do I have a spouse who won't support a budget or the ability to do these things?

Take a hard look at the stories that you're using and the state that you're in, and play those roles out. Watch yourself on that movie screen. Look at that actor and ask yourself, "Is what I'm seeing true?" It's probably somewhat compelling, unless you're the only audience member going, "I'm not buying it. That's a bunch of bull!"

Beneath all that, deep down, there's a place inside you that wants to scream out, "Wait a minute, I could win and hold myself as if I'd won a gold medal."

Let's think about that for a second. How would you have to position your body when you've done something spectacular and standing up on the podium? Imagine it. Your chest is held high, your shoulders are back, you're breathing deeply. You have a huge smile on your face, your eyes are alive. You've just had a transformative moment.

Now, take another look at those questions on the previous pages. Turn these questions around and ask yourself how. How can you get yourself motivated? How can you take steps to live the life you are meant to live? What steps can you do to start to take action NOW?

TURNING WHY INTO HOW

Now, let's go back to how you are expressing yourself in your appointment schedule. Are you using words that are, in effect, self-defeating words that allow the brain to keep on churning but aren't allowing you to take action? Instead of asking a *why* that doesn't inspire you to take action, maybe you could ask yourself *how*.

Don't ask why you're not living your dreams. Ask instead what you need to do to be able start making them happen. How can you do something just for today to start turning them into reality?

Next, are you focused on the barriers? The defeat? The shackles that are tying you down? Your focus really matters. By now you've come up with a list of values that matter to you. There's a saying "Don't tell me what you value, show me where you spend your money and I'll show you what you value." That's where your focus should live. How can you make values happen, not, why aren't they happening now?

Here are some questions to ask yourself about your values:

- Do they represent an action?
- Do they represent gratitude, giving back to others?
- Do they represent love and connection to others?
- Does fulfilling these values matter deeply to you?

Let's take your work experience as an example. How you show up should match the values that are important to you. Do you show up to excite? Do you have gratitude for this person or people being in your life? Do you show up in a way that allows you to serve them? If you don't—if you're at a job you don't like and resent—you'll make that the excuse for why you're behaving poorly or not succeeding as you'd like.

This is also true about money. Too many people live by the rule that, "In order for me to be happy I have to make X amount of money". What happens if that rule is in conflict with your values? What if in order to make X amount of money you have to work really hard, and this conflicts with your intention to spend quality family time or prevents you from being able to spend time on that hobby that's your true passion?

The usual way of thinking is to ask the *why* question. Why should you have to give up doing the things you want to do for the things you have to do?

What we don't realize is that asking the *how* question can lead to results. How can you build a bridge that is orchestrated to allow everyone to play together to create a beautiful symphony? How can you earn enough to support yourself and do the things you want to experience in life? How can you live a life you love?

Most successful entrepreneurs, regardless of background, age, sex, credential or experience, understand that effective business building strategies are only part of the equation. They recognize that most of the results come from an empowered psychology that allows them to follow through and apply the strategies that create growth.

A lot of people, however, don't see the importance of this. Mike Koenigs, the author of *Make, Market, Launch IT*, expresses this point with these words: "I'm too tired, by the time I get home I just don't have the energy to start on me." Great, I understand that.

A more effective strategy might go something like this. Reverse the order. Start your day working on yourself, and then show up for what comes next. This takes us back to Napoleon Hill's basic question: What are you willing to give in order to get the results you desire? What is your "give to get"? Maybe this means getting up forty-five minutes earlier in the day to spend time on yourself.

Before you start your day ask yourself, "What is my purpose today? What is the best part of my day today?" If you come up short, don't start your day until you come up with strong answers for that.

What do you do with that time? Maybe it's devotion. Maybe it's meditation time. Maybe it's physical conditioning. Maybe it's time to implement your dreams. After that you can go on with the rest of your day, go out into the rest of the world that is waiting for you to take action. At the end of the day you could go to bed forty-five minutes earlier without having added any time to your schedule.

You have the talent! It comes down to the psychology, what it means to you and why. What is the meaning you're giving to this?

Listen to the metaphors you're using. Are your default response words that don't serve you to take action like, "I can't do it, I'm tired, I'm exhausted, I worked hard and deserve a break…" or "this is too heavy, this is weighing me down like a ton of bricks"?

Try this instead. Use metaphors that are empowering. Change the meaning. Change the language. How much more powerful to think instead, "This is a bridge to my future prosperity."

I know that doing this isn't easy, and goes back to the saying, "The only place success comes before work is in the dictionary." All dreams are outside of our comfort zone, and the price that we must pay in order to achieve those dreams is to get uncomfortable. But the system to implement them is easy. All you need to do is to build the habits and consistently use them in order to bring your dreams to fruition.

Yes, it takes real discipline and real work, and—don't forget— you can also make this process fun. You can encourage your growth to happen in a joyful way. That's when the most memories happen. You tend to remember the things that are worth doing.

TIME ISN'T THE PROBLEM TAKEAWAYS:

1. This is my plan for today.
2. These are the most important events of my day that I am starting with and making sure they lead my day. This is the other stuff that fits after the most important.

LOSE THIS NASTY HABIT

"A person who doubts himself is like a man who would enlist in the ranks of his enemies and bear arms against himself."

—Alexandre Dumas

Neuro-Linguistic Programming (NLP) would say that you think 60,000-80,000 thoughts a day. Most of those thoughts are in your head. How much of that is negative self-talk?

Too much, unfortunately. Too often you go through your life blissfully unaware of how you are your own worst enemy by beating yourself up with language abuse. Thoughts that, even if they're not expressed in these exact words, express the feelings of:

- "I'm not good enough"
- "I can't do it"
- "I'm stupid"

- "I'm unlovable"
- "I'll never make it"
- "I'm not worthy"

These thoughts are the reasons that hold you back, and as damaging as if an army had unleashed all its weapons on you.

Fortunately, there's a way to combat this: repetition.

New, positive thoughts can replace that negative talk, but only through time and repetition. As Gandhi said: "Your beliefs become your thoughts. Your thoughts become your words. Your words become your actions. Your actions become your habits. Your habits become your values. Your values become your destiny."

Here is how I put repetition into practice. I have created a collection of positive quotes, and I look at them first thing every morning. These quotes help me create the repetition of taking action, being persistent, and being purposeful in my language. This repetitive practice has become a habit that keeps me on track as I take on the rest of the day.

Here are a few examples:

- I am going to keep The Four Agreements just for today
    - Be impeccable with my word
    - Take nothing personally
    - Make no assumptions
    - Do my best
- Activate the Peaceful Warrior. Embrace the silence. Embrace the space between
- Always be on-time and complete meetings on-time
- Five disciplines that were an integral part of what Jesus practiced during His earthly walk:
    - Practicing Solitude — Spending time alone with God

   - Experiencing Prayer — Speaking with God
   - Applying Scripture — Preparing for the challenges that were yet to come
   - Abiding in God's Unconditional Love — Proceeding with confidence, grounded in trust
   - Maintaining Supportive Relationships — Sharing His vulnerability, from Servant Leader by Ken Blanchard.
- "I will not let a man walk through my mind with dirty feet." – Gandhi
- "If you keep using your low points as an excuse, they will prevent you from living a life that matters." – Chad Cooper
- "Most people struggle with life balance simply because they haven't paid the price to decide what is really important to them." – Stephen Covey
- My Daily Bread & Bedside Prayer
- There is a difference between wishing for a thing and being ready to receive it.
- What's wrong is always available, and so is What's Right! At this time, I also go over a list of seven statements that resonate with me:
   - I am happy to be me.
   - I am me. I am right here.
   - This is really me.
   - I do it.   I decide.
   - The world is a reflection of me.
   - I am source.
   - My strength comes from within, and God is within me.

If this idea resonates with you, it's easy to do. You don't have to use my favorite quotes. Find ones that mean something special to you.

There are many Internet sites that are filled with positive affirmations. Take advantage of them. Create your own habit around them.

I use this daily practice to structure myself, to be purposeful and intentional, and to surround myself with people who are more empowered.

By the way, that's also why I don't watch the news on television. There's nothing in the NEWS that inspires me. Generally, I find the news to be a textbook example of negative repetition, in how to justify why my life doesn't suck very much only because this person's life is worse.

It's a low quality societal standard to allow ourselves to stay imprisoned and not do something about it. It's as if to say, "You think your shackles are awful? This person's got shackles and they're hanging off of a cliff. They're in much more pain." We justify and say, "I guess I'm not in such a dire situation."

What this also does is mask what's real for you. The reality is that you hold the key. Turn off the TV and go do something that excites you. Play out the roles that give you passion. In my case, it's the roles of *Superdad, Abundance,* and *Radiance Worshipper.* What are yours? Do them. Take action.

When you do, those actions turn into habits. Then those habits will become your values, and those values will become your destiny.

For people who are struggling with the beliefs of *I don't have enough, there's not enough to go around*, and *I wish I could do better,* I recommend the writings of Don Miguel Ruiz, author of *The Four Agreements.* I get inspiration from him myself. As I mentioned above, one of the quotes that reoccurs on my schedule every four days or so says, "Just for today I'm going to uphold the Four Agreements."

What I love about *The Four Agreements* is that if you implement them you can't fail. The first agreement, "Be Impeccable With Your

Word," goes back to those 60,000-80,000 thoughts you have every day. How many of those thoughts have real purpose? Your impeccability starts with being intentional with your language. One way to have that show up for you is in the integrity of the subject line of your schedule. Is there strength in the purpose within the language of your schedule events?

To me, the second agreement, "Don't Make Assumptions" means that I'm listening before I'm forming my thoughts. I'm hearing what the other person is telling me without the autobiographical language saying, "I did it this way, therefore you need to do things my way to get to the same result" or "Do you even need me to give a response?" I'm creating the space to allow that person to get their words out. Making no assumptions means that I'm stopping. I'm giving myself time to digest and then respond rather than react thoughtlessly.

The third agreement, "Don't Take Anything Personally", applies not only to the negative, but to the positive as well. If somebody compliments you, say thank you and let those words flow right through you. If somebody says something negative, thank them and let their message dissipate and go through you. If you hold onto something and take it personally, you're no longer being present. If it's positive, that's preventing you from letting anything else good come into your life. If it's negative, you become so focused on that thought that you can't see something great that might be going on somewhere else.

The fourth agreement is "Always Do Your Best." As long as you do your best, you can't fail. You always win. This principle really allows you to celebrate and say, "I did my best and that was good enough, now let me try again." The cycle then circles back to the agreement of being impeccable with your word.

UPGRADE YOUR BRAIN

All computers get software upgrades. It's what makes them work more efficiently, more productively. Why not let your brain get a software upgrade too? Why would you use an old operating system when there's a new one that's readily available? You have the ability to upgrade your operating system. What's preventing you from doing that?

How do you upgrade your brain? If you don't have the financial means, there's this place called the library where you can access things for free. There are tons of resources on the internet. You can listen to TED Talks for free. You can watch YouTube. There are online universities nowadays. Low cost community college courses. If coming to one of my events for whatever cost saves your marriage, gets you to that dream vacation, or allows you to spend quality time with a family member… what price would you pay to make it happen? There's an abundant amount of information that people are providing for you to be able to do this. Where is this continuing education scheduled on your calendar?

Be resourceful and do not let the limitations that you think are there, those limiting beliefs, get in the way of your taking action.

TIME ISN'T THE PROBLEM TAKEAWAYS:

1. I will use repetition in this way to positively impact my life.
2. I will turn them into habits by doing this.

FUEL FOR THE SOUL

Are you a person or a robot?

Don't be so quick to answer. Oftentimes we just go along with the routines; we just go through the motions. Do we actually stop and focus before we go into a meeting, walk into church, sit down to dinner? Are we being impeccable before we walk in setting the stage — the stage for ourselves?

I like to use the acronym of FUEL — **Focus, Urgency, Energy and Leverage** — as a way of gauging whether you're in the proper mindset for whatever activity you're about to do.

FOCUS

When you show up, are you focused, present? What is the purpose of this appointment, this opportunity? If you are suffering the loss of a loved one, are you focusing on the memories of the years you had with this person or the loss of the years you won't have with this person? Are you focused on things that are missing or things that you already have?

Are you focused on moving forward or away from what you really want? Abraham Lincoln got it right about focus, "Happiness is an inside job".

URGENCY

What's the urgency? Are you operating in reaction mode, or have you been purposeful in planning this out? How important is something to you? The goal would be to work on things that are important but not urgent to you. In other words, the goal is to be purposeful and not to procrastinate. Most people don't do what's important and procrastinate simply because they have not linked the purpose of what they really want into the subject line of the event they are about to undertake.

It's really just about asking the urgency. This doesn't mean that everything has to be urgent or not urgent. It's not about reactive versus proactive. If the intention is that there is no urgency for this time, have you given enough space to do other actions or are you trying to do too much in a compressed amount of time? Are you piling your plate so full that your urgency is causing you to lose your point of focus?

As an example, if you have a meeting scheduled for an hour, and have about fifteen minutes' worth of urgent items to discuss, put those items on the agenda first. That ensures that what needs to be done gets done, leaving you the rest of the time to handle the less urgent matters with ease and less stress.

ENERGY

What is your energy level before you go in, on a scale of 0 to 10? If it's less than 7.5 and you're struggling, this is why. If you don't have the energy, if you're not feeling empowered, stop. Do something to shake yourself and raise your personal energy, to enable you to be present when you show up. This can be done through using empowering language to amplify your sense of purpose.

LEVERAGE

If there are actions that need to happen, where can you resource other tools, people, time, money or whatever, in order to spend your time on things that matter most? What will it cost you not to take this action? What will your life look like a year from now if you do take action? What do you need to do to make yourself feel successful?

When you leverage, where can you use other people or technology or automation to help you accomplish your goals? You then could focus on the things that are more important.

As an example of what I mean, let's look at how a professional life coach can use leverage to grow his business. Let's say the coach charges $200 an hour and wants to hire an assistant. The assistant's rate is $15 an hour. If the coach hires the assistant, his effective worth is now $185 an hour, as he has determined that the assistant would be doing $15 an hour worth of work.

That is a simple math equation, but the coach might have a hard time getting over that understanding because it's very emotional. This comes from a fear based mindset in which the coach might think he's taking the money away from himself. He's not looking at the larger picture. Having an assistant might make the coach more effective and might give the coach more time to attract new clients. The additional clients would certainly cover the costs of the assistant. He might even be able to raise his rates to offset the costs.

TIME ISN'T THE PROBLEM TAKEAWAYS:

1. This is how I used FUEL to gauge my mindset.
2. This is how I will use FUEL to be more effective.

STRATEGY THREE:

HONOR THE SPIRITUAL

YOU ARE DIVINE

I struggled with the idea of talking about a "higher power" in these pages. This is not meant to be a book about religion, and I didn't want the main points to be lost on those who might turn away at any mention of the word "God". Yet the subject is too important to ignore, as I believe it's impossible to truly know your purpose in life without addressing your relationship to the divine.

Scholars and religious experts have poured over this question for centuries. When I thought about it from the perspective of God and energy, I was able to make a connection that has forever impacted my life in immeasurable ways. I believe we are all connected energetically, and here is how I account for a "higher being".

THE THREE LEVELS OF MASCULINE AND FEMININE

An incredible and powerful life coach, Ben Austin, gave me one of the most insightful gifts I have ever received to date aside from my faith. He believes that everything is about feminine and masculine energy and in which levels of that energy we are choosing to live.

Differences in temperament between men and women are not necessarily a function of biological differences. Numerous studies have shown that temperaments result from differences in socialization and the cultural expectations held for each sex.

David Deida, who has written extensively on spirituality and sexuality, also has defined this concept by stating that masculine and feminine energies can be broken down into three distinct levels.

MASCULINE LEVELS

Level One is hyper masculine. I like to call him the "enemy warrior". This is the guy who wants to get in everyone's face and kick ass. You know the type; the grunting guy in the gym overcompensating in his physical form likely because he is afraid internally. Old world tradition would describe him as the man bringing home the bacon, but also expressing intimidation, threats, and emotional violence. The energy level here is that of creating an energy state, but only for himself.

Level Two is "pussy boy". Yes, the term is meant to shock you, and just because of the shocking language we may desire to soften this type of person by calling him the "person pleaser", "sensitive flow boy", or someone who practices "boy psychology". This level is associated with political correctness, doing things the right and proper way. This is a person who doesn't rock the boat too much. He accepts other people's rules and lives in the effect of their decisions. The energy here is a sucking of energy state.

Level Three is the "present man" or "Warrior of Love". This is the man who knows his

Mission, has freedom, acts through love. He is at cause in his life, gets what he accepts, and lives by his standards through love. He is the "hero knight" or as I call him "King Arthur" if you are familiar with the fable story. He will take up his mission regardless of acceptance or rejection by society, because he knows his purpose and reason for being. He is able to create or use energy at his discretion.

Looking at these definitions, it's obvious that the optimum goal for a man would want to live in his Level Three masculinity. However, a man might become confused or stuck when he has one

element of Level Three, but is missing other pieces of the formula. For example, a man may take on a mission out of pressure to please another person, or frankly out of choice initially. However, in the process he will become imprisoned along the way. He may be living in the false belief of, "I have to do this or that" vs. "I get to…" or "I choose to" and miss the opportunity to combine his mission with freedom.

When a man is not in Level Three, a woman can pick this up immediately. I have watched Ben demonstrate this to countless people; a woman can sense in a heartbeat when a man believes he is clever enough to fool others but lacks congruence in action.

FEMININE LEVELS

Level One feminine is "queen diva" or "perfect housewife". This is the woman who must keep the spotlight on her no matter the circumstances. Again, you know the type; the woman so overcome with grief at a funeral that she takes the focus off the person in the casket. Often, however, she shows up as the perfect being on the surface and behind the scenes is trading her sex for power in the marriage. They tend to judge themselves through external factors like a level one man.

Level Two feminine is "butch". This is another strong word meant to shock. A subtler term often used is "working girl". A gross exaggeration of this is the woman who behaves, looks, dresses and stands like a man. She uses rules and politics to win. She checks her feminine at the board room door because she believes it doesn't belong in the business world.

Level Three is "radiance". This is where a woman wants to live. She is healthy and expressive. This woman offers her divine radiance in service of her partner and the world. She desires to penetrate the world with her truth and love. Don't mistake this for always calm and peaceful waves of love, for it is not politically correct, it is truth.

Those in Level Two of masculine or feminine may be offended by these definitions because the softened edges come off in the truth of these observations. Often a woman will go to Levels One or Two when a man is not living in his Level Three greatness. When a woman doesn't feel there is a masculine presence guarding her kingdom, she believes she is not safe to live in her radiance unless she takes on the qualities of a Level One person.

CONNECTING WITH A HIGHER SOURCE

What does this have to do with God? How we act reflects on our connection to our higher self. When we are serving our mission and are free in that decision, we are present, connected in our soul to ourselves, others, and the universe. This is about going beyond the visual, auditory, and feeling, and into the things we can't explain scientifically or by instruments. This is where we may enter the realm of "miracle".

We see examples of this in society all the time. Take the man who lifts a car off another person in an accident. He doesn't do it from Level Two or One. He connects with his divine and his soul, and this connection gives him the strength to do what some would call impossible.

I've asked both men and women, "When you connect with your higher self, your God, are you able to do it in Level One or Two?" The answer every time was, "Mentally and energetically I need to be in Level Three."

Those answers helped me realize that God gives us the gift of choice to be whatever level we choose, but to connect our soul with the world and God, we need to energetically meet him in our radiance and presence.

When I am present as a man, I am connected to my son, to my wife, and to the world. I have absolute certainty in my mission. I am free. I am love. I am significant. I feel and experience growth and desire to contribute this to the world. In essence, in Level Three masculine, I am meeting all of my needs, and only through this can I truly connect to God. This is how I know there is a higher being. I feel the incredible energy force that otherwise I cannot explain in my life. I have faith and I experience the divine every day when I choose willingly to connect through total presence.

Abraham Lincoln said, "*Nearly all men can stand adversity, but if you want to test a man's character, give him power.*" A Level One man will abuse that power, a Level Two man will run away from its intensity, but a Level Three man, connected to the universe, will own that power, and his character will align to the values of his God. For the feminine, the Level One will be used to manipulate others for her gain.

It's not easy to get to the bottom of who you really are and your purpose in life. As an example, recently I was coaching a client whom I saw as a Level Two woman. She came to me for help because she felt she was struggling and needed to make more money. She's a single mother with a one-year-old daughter. In order to reach her goals, she needed to change, but I wasn't sure she understood how her own self-limiting beliefs were impeding her growth.

I asked her to imagine the effect her situation was having on her daughter's life. "How's your daughter going to thrive in life when she's learning from you to settle and give up? Is that the legacy you want to teach her? Is that who you want to be? Do you want your daughter to grow up and believe she doesn't deserve much and has to settle because that's what her mom did?"

She broke down in tears. It was hard to watch, but I knew she had to connect with that deepest part of her in order to see how her actions were hurting her and her daughter. She needed to get beyond the Level

Two butch and the political correctness she believed was serving her and her daughter.

This is true for everyone: Until it hurts, you're not going to change long term; you're going to hold onto an identity of "this is who I am". Until you identify with who that other person is—the one who operates from radiance and higher self—and it becomes present and not future tense based, you'll continue to repeat those patterns.

You have to ask yourself the question: What's it costing me to live here?

When my client chooses to live in her Level Three radiance, she then realizes that God has given her a spring well right inside her soul. That strength is enough to influence her daughter to be whoever she really is and not fear hiding it from the world. I offer that she also might benefit from a masculine presence to protect the kingdom so she can be radiant and not have to be the knight at the same time. Energy is balancing the masculine and feminine and there was no masculine energy to counterbalance in her life, hence part of her struggle.

HOW TO LIVE IN LEVEL THREE

Doesn't the idea that you live in your most divine, most giving, most enlightened self all the time sound wonderful?

Yeah, it sounds great. It's also unrealistic. To live in Level Three all the time, would make you a saint, and no man or woman is that perfect. I bet even the Pope has his off moments when he reacts with anger or resentment or jealousy or envy—just like the rest of us.

In reality, we flow in and out of these levels all the time. All you have to do is ask my wife or son and they'll give you a laundry list of the times I've had bad days and sunk to classic Level One behavior. But because I've created and made habits —and that includes putting it on my calendar — to be aware of when I make these slips, I'm able to correct these impulses before I do something I know I'll later regret.

This was brought home to me on a recent vacation trip I took with my family. We were on a boat with a large group of people, all traveling to a throwback island where we'd be without cars and many modern conveniences. Traveling with us was a quartet of swarthy, young college-aged boys who looked like they were from the Middle East. About halfway through the journey, these boisterous guys started singing in a strange foreign language. Loudly. I mean, VERY loudly.

I glanced around at my fellow travelers and could see a sense of unease grow among them. I imagined these boat mates were all thinking what I was thinking: *Who the #$*! do they think they are? Don't they realize we're all here to relax? This is America, guys, and you have to have respect.*

Things got a bit worse when a few minutes later, one of the boys took out a whistle and began tooting to the rhythm of the song. Again, VERY LOUDLY.

At that point I'd had it. The Level One hyper-masculine side of me wanted to jump down their throats and tell them to shut up. Another part of me wouldn't have minded pushing them overboard as well.

Then I stopped myself and asked, "Is any of that really going to accomplish the outcome I want here?"

Asking myself that question was like breaking a spell. I was able to step back from the Level One emotional fury and take another look at what was around me. Instead of potential terrorists, I saw instead a group of young boys who were having fun and blissfully unaware of their surroundings.

Then I asked myself another question: What would a Level Three man do? With this mindset, I then approached the group. With a smile on my face, I said, "Hey, you guys are having a lot of fun but you're obviously not from around here. Did you all come together?"

The question stunned them. I had interrupted them, but I hadn't challenged them. Instead of getting Level One confrontation, they got

Level Three acceptance. I could see their faces soften, so I went on. "I know you guys are having fun, and we all want to have fun and the whistle is probably a bit overboard here. But I'm really curious. What are you singing and in what language?" This friendly attitude welcomed them and in the process made them aware that not everyone else was enjoying what they were doing.

Long story short, the leader of the group motioned to the guy with the whistle and told him to stop. "These people want to relax," he told his friends. "We can do this later."

I ended up running into the group a few days later on the island. They hugged me and asked if they could take a picture with me—a happy outcome to what could have been a distressing situation. All because I chose to be the cause that I wanted, rather than living in the effect of their behavior. It's not their behavior that made me make a decision. *I* chose, and I chose to live in their Level Three presence.

I admit that it took a lot of practice and a lot of habit building for me to get to this place. Most people might have reacted differently. Sure there could have been the hyper-masculine Level One approach. Mostly likely that would have led to tempers being raised, as the boys would have lowered themselves to their own Level One presence. Whether the argument would have devolved to outright fighting is anyone's guess, but you get the picture. Going toe-to-toe in the heat of the moment usually doesn't end well.

Actually a more typical reaction was the one that nearly everyone else on that boat had—going to their Level Two identity. Literally they didn't want to "rock the boat" by making a scene. This is what I mean by Level Two being the "pussy boy". It's the fear-based *I have an opportunity to change this, but oh, man, I don't have the courage or I'm afraid what would happen* reaction. They don't step into the opportunity. They run away from it. While these people avoided making a scene, they also experienced being unfulfilled by not getting the peace and quiet they desired. They were not serving their mission.

But by rising to my Level Three presence, the young men were inspired to rise to theirs as well. Everyone benefited from the process.

LEVEL THREE AND THE DIVINE

Where did God enter my life? God never left my life. However, I put Him in the proverbial closet when I lived in Level One masculinity. This was when I was saying, in effect, "I'm great, I got this. You stay there; I can handle this without you." This was a textbook example of the hyper-masculine at work. "I'll just force this thing into submission!"

But that was me getting in my own way. It's only when I stopped and realized, "It's not up to me. I have to be willing to let everything go," that I embraced my Level Three masculinity and allowed God into my life.

When I say everything, I'm not talking just about the material possessions. I mean I'm willing to let everything—even my family—go by the wayside. It's not what I want or wish. But if God took everything away from me, I'd be okay. Eckhart Tolle, Jesus, and the Dalai Lama would say we are not to cling to others so tightly that it prevents us from being present because we are holding so tightly to the past or future that we cannot "be". If we do, we risk living in Level Two.

When we leave our radiance or masculine presence and begin living in a lesser level of energy, we are not trusting that we are enough. I choose not to live like that. I believe that we were given unlimited power, and that the power comes from our higher self.

We are here to enrich and take in what the universe has to offer. At the same time, we decide which level of energy to live within. Our higher power gave us this free will, but there are consequences of not living within the laws of each level. If a man believes that living as a man who knows his mission is something he cannot uphold long-term, then he's entered Level Two who is afraid he is not enough. If a woman believes her radiance cannot be sustained and she goes masculine to try to force the events in her life, this causes a fallout as well.

I say that we always have choice. There's a part of me that says, "God is always going to care for me. God will never put me in a position that is more than I can bear."

There was a point somewhere in my life where I realized I was always sending a text, "God, this is what I need, I'm in trouble. If you could just see your way to help me in this one instance today, I'll never ask anything—until tomorrow." But that was always a one-way conversation.

Then I started going through some exercises. One resource I would really recommend is Eckhart Tolle for the Western Hemisphere Mindset. He's best known for his book *The Power of Now,* but his second book *A New Earth: Awakening to Your Life's Purpose,* really hit home for me. It was after reading this that I was struck by the realization that I was approaching life from the false perspective of the hyper-masculine.

A story he told in the book really hit home for me. For years, he'd felt a certain smug sense of satisfaction by being the guy who said he was trading in his fancy car for a bicycle. Then one day as he was riding his bike, he stopped at a street sign next to a person driving a Mercedes.

"Look at me," he told the man. "I traded my gas guzzling car for an efficient, ecologically sound bicycle. I'm more present than you."

To his surprise, the man answered back, "No, you're not, Idiot. Your ego's still in the way. You think you're superior because you're riding a bicycle, but your ego is making you less again. It's not about the vehicle. It's about you. You've got to let go of the ego."

He was right. Tolle had to learn to keep his own ego and fear on the side, and that's a lesson we all can learn. For me, there's an interesting balance because I wouldn't consider myself a humble person, but it's not because I tell the world, "Look at what I did." Instead I say, "Look at what God is doing through me." I've taken away the ego. It's not me. It's me acting out the blessings that God's putting in front of me.

When you say you want patience or prosperity, be careful what you ask for because He's not going to just give you patience. God's going to give you an opportunity to exhibit patience. He's going to put a challenge in your way and say, "Action." You then get the opportunity to choose, to decide whether to be the Level One person and fight or be the Level Three master that breathes in, connects with your presence or radiance, and lets the patience pass through you.

When you say things to yourself such as "I don't have enough" or "what about me?" you are living in Level Two, and that's when you get in trouble. You feel the weight of the world is on your shoulders and you're being asked to take care of everyone around you when you don't feel like you have even enough to take care of yourself. Those are the times when you have to seek out that Level Three energy, to get present, let go of the ego, look around and go, "There's some energy. It's all around me and I can accept it."

There's a story told about the Buddha. Buddha was well known for his ability to respond to evil with good. A man who knew about his reputation traveled miles and miles to test him. When the man arrived, he stood before Buddha and verbally abused him constantly. He insulted him. He challenged him. He did everything he could to offend this great master.

Yet Buddha was unmoved. He turned to the man and said, "May I ask you a question?"

The man responded gruffly, "Well what?"

Buddha said to the man, "If someone gives you a gift and you decline to accept it, to whom does the gift belong?"

The angry man replied, "It belongs to the person who offered it."

Buddha smiled. "That is correct. So if I decline to accept your abuse, does it not then still belong to you?"

The man was speechless and walked away sheepishly.

If somebody is giving you aggression or anger, it's usually because you're just mirroring what's already inside of you. You can't give what you don't first possess yourself. You can just simply say the frustration and anger doesn't have to be mine. I don't have to resist it. Resistance requires even more energy. Don't resist it. Acknowledge that it's there and let it dissipate through you. When you dissipate and disown that negativity, that action also allows the other person to release their negativity and not have to own it any longer.

A WELLSPRING OF ENERGY

So, how does this relate to an extraordinary life? I say that when you make the declaration to connect to your Level Three, energy aligns and you tap into the "bat phone line" directly to God. When I am connected to my higher self, I am present, living my mission, and free in that pursuit.

Each day I look at my life and ask myself, "If I got hit by a truck do I have regrets?" I keep working on the belief that my answer is always going to be, "No". I wake up each day asking myself what I can accomplish. I don't worry about not having enough energy; I have an infinite supply from my eternal, internal spring well.

I also don't need weekends to "recharge". I've discovered along the way that my week is no longer divided by weekday and weekend. It's just each day. Saturday? Wednesday? It doesn't matter.

When you stop subscribing to weekday versus weekend, you're on a trajectory to really feel fulfilled, really feel passionate. This is because you're no longer living for the future, you're embracing right now, the present.

One of the gifts that Eckhart Tolle brought us is the concept of always being present— living in the present moment—versus living in the past or future. If you treat every day as an opportunity, you start taking opportunities and you become resourceful. This is the highest example of living a Level Three life.

MAKING SPIRITUALITY PRACTICAL

I firmly believe that when you're coming from your place of spirituality, you find a way to integrate it into every area of your life. You come from a place where your energy level is open and abundant, as opposed to coming from a place of lack, where you feel there's not enough to go around. What ends up happening is that more actually comes back to you in return.

This shows up in my volunteer work. I consider myself a "servant leader", in that I lead a group that does charity work in Guatemala every year. Organizing these journeys is fulfilling to me, but just as importantly, this trip creates the opportunity for others to rise to their Level Three as well. For example, one of our missions is providing medical care for impoverished people who live in hard to reach villages. I don't know one end of a needle from the other, but the doctors and nurses I get to volunteer for this trip sure do. They have expertise in an area where I don't, and this trip enables them to express their gifts and have their own sense of fulfillment realized.

Most importantly for me, however, is the effect this has on my son. Because he sees how I act, he'll grow up with the mindset that there's more than enough to go around and be encouraged to rise to this Level Three presence. He won't be living in survival. He'll have the opportunity to create stability and move into a success that he'll define by his own standards.

In the next section, I'll put all of these ideas from Steps One, Two and Three together, and show you how scheduling your time smartly and productively will transform your stress into success and lead you to a life that truly matters.

TIME ISN'T THE PROBLEM TAKEAWAYS:

1. I currently live in this level of feminine or masculine energy.
2. This is how I can live in Level Three from this point forward. I would need to let go of these things in order to step into Level Three.
3. This one thing is possible from this position. I can take action on it today by doing this.

STRATEGY FOUR

WORKING WITH THE RULE OF 168

WHERE DID THAT WEEK GO?

"Reduce your plan to writing. The moment you complete this, you will have definitely given concrete form to the intangible desire."
—Napoleon Hill

I began this book with the notion that there are 168 hours in the week. Don't be upset with yourself if this was news to you. Most people never get past the idea of there being twenty-four hours in a day, let alone think about an entire week's worth of hours.

I'll let you in on a little secret. The people who do know there are 168 hours in the week—and who honor that knowledge—are the people who know how to make the most of their time and their lives. It's how they're able to do the things they do, and why other people can't. How did Tim Farris figure out the four-hour work week as an example? How are people like Sir Richard Branson able to live a life of ever expanding experiences, and yet still be able to execute the responsibilities to maintain what they've created?

They've learned how to manage their time effectively. These people also are masters at knowing themselves and their purpose in the ways that were outlined in the first three sections of this book.

This section deals with the nitty gritty and practical ways to make sure you make the most efficient and productive use of your time.

Let's get down to the basics. 168 hours. That seems like a large number. But is it really? We'll start by seeing how you spend your time right now. Now, I'm not a math whiz, but I'm capable of simple calculations, like this.

The typical person sleeps eight hours a night. Eight hours multiplied by seven is fifty-six. Taking that off the top leaves 112 hours.

Next up is to calculate the second largest block of your time; the hours spent on your job. Whether you work for somebody, you're an entrepreneur or a stay-at-home mom, for the purpose of this exercise we're going to assume a typical forty-hour work week. Subtract that and that leaves us with 72 hours.

Seventy-two hours. What do you do with all that time? We all have various roles, various obligations. How much of your time is spent working on your passions, doing the things that honor the purpose of your life? How much of that time is spent procrastinating, doing mindless activities like watching TV, surfing the net or playing video games? How much of that time is frittered away on other chores or tasks that are not planned correctly?

Hmm...no wonder you never get the feeling that you're on the road to success.

You've probably never given much thought to how you spend your time. Here's a way how to figure that out. Make a list of the things you do during a typical week. Keep the categories broad. Washing dishes and cleaning the house, for example, would be part of the category you can call *Beautifying My Environment.* Add everything up and then divide each category by 168. That number will tell you the percentage of time you're spending performing each of those roles.

AN EXERCISE IN TIME MANAGEMENT

Let's say, for example, you've decided that spending more time with your spouse is important to you. In my opinion, I believe that couples who have great relationships ought to spend, on average, sixteen hours a week together. I consider that a valid amount of time to honor the most important person in our lives whom we love. That's roughly ten percent of the week. It's an admirable number to target. When you realize this is only about two and a half hours a day, this hardly seems like any time at all.

By the way, I'm talking quantity of time, not quality of time. How the time is spent is not the issue here.

Do most people reach this target? Let's look at the reality for a lot of people. Since most people work during the week, time with the spouse is usually put off to the weekend. But for two-thirds of us, that time commitment is just a thought in our heads. *I want to spend the time*, we tell ourselves. Is that what really happens?

Again, because we work during the week, a lot of chores or tasks like grocery shopping, going to the dry cleaners, getting our hair done, going clothes shopping, cleaning the house, or even playing golf with buddies, get put off to the weekend. There goes that spouse time.

Perhaps, some of these activities are done with the spouse. Perhaps, you make time for a Saturday night movie or dinner date, and you spend time together at church on Sunday. But most likely those activities are shared with friends or family and might not count as just spouse time.

When all is said and done, that grand plan for sixteen hours realistically starts to look more like four hours every week.

Four hours. That's 3.6 percent of your week. If you both feel that's sufficient, fine. Forget about what everybody else says you should be doing. If that's the percentage that works for both of you, honor that, work with that, and then go on from there.

But perhaps that doesn't sound like much time to you. You tell yourself, "I'm sleeping twenty percent of my week, and I'm spending about twenty to thirty percent of my week working, and she gets a measly scrap of 3.6 percent? My gosh, I'm cheating my wife out of loving her! That seems like a miniscule number."

What do you do? If you've stayed with me up to this point you already know the answer. That's right. You put your spouse on the calendar. You vow to make amends and to create that quality time that will put the purpose back into your marriage.

But wait. There's more.

If you don't do *all* the steps, you set yourself up to fail because you've set this lofty goal based on rules in order to feel like you're winning. It's not enough just to pencil in the spouse on the calendar. You need to go back to the purpose behind why you're putting your spouse on the calendar in the first place.

What language are you using in this scenario? Are you using limp language in your subject header? At this point, I hope not. On a scale of zero to ten, your descriptive words should be a ten. You should be using the visual, the auditory and the kinesthetic to really create the identity, the role and experience you want to have. You want to have great intentions. You set a goal of say, eight or twelve hours with this person. You go for a hike, you go shopping together, you go golfing together, or you go to a movie together.

How do you show up for your spouse at that point? Do you show up as Superman or do you show up as defeated and never live up to the expectation that this person wants? As a man, are you showing up in your Level Three presence, or are you already in your head working on what's going to happen the rest of the week and how you're supposed to fit in your work commitments because you're supposed to be doing this with your spouse? If you're a woman, are you showing up loving, passionate, playful, joyful, or sexy? Are you speaking just the truth, or the truth through love? Are you showing up in your Level Three feminine radiance?

What about your descriptions of the activities themselves? Do you use the words *going on a hike* or *delightful outdoor adventure*? If you're going to the supermarket with your spouse, is that opportunity a *run for errands* or a *magic moments jaunt?*

TIME SWAPPING

Let's say you believe four hours is not enough. You want to do more. Here's how to find that extra time you may believe you don't have. This is the same method used by people who are experts in time management, like Richard Branson, Warren Buffet, Bill Gates, and Tony Robbins.

Let's say you want to add two more hours, to bring the total up to six hours a week.

Go back to that list you made of where you historically spend your time. Simply say, "Where can I borrow that time from the other roles that I'm playing?" As Napoleon Hill writes, "What are you willing to give in return for the result that you desire?" What's your "give to get"?

Perhaps that time can come from your sleep. You can tell yourself that you'd be willing to go to bed a little later twice a week. You can do that for two hours, one hour for each day. You're honoring the 168-hour rule. You're not adding to time that doesn't exist. You're managing your wants in the time that you have.

If you were truly honest with yourself and made a list of all the time you need to do the things you want to do during a week, you might end up with 190 or 200 hours' worth of activities. No wonder you have stress. No wonder you believe there's never any time to do anything. There isn't!

But there certainly can be, if you make the effort to borrow from one of the other roles, and ask the hard questions:

- What's my give to get?
- What is the price I'm willing to pay?
- Am I willing to work fewer hours in my career?
- Am I willing to get less sleep?
- Am I willing to exercise less for this?
- Am I willing to pay somebody else to do something I'm already doing for myself?

Don't get limited by what you're willing to pay as just time or money. You might also be willing to give up a limiting belief that's held you back. For example, you might have to give up the belief, "I'll never get it done", if that's keeping you from a household task. Or you might have to give up the belief, "I'm too old to learn", if that's keeping you from learning a new skill.

You also might be willing to leverage and ask for help. If you say, "I need to hire somebody to do this," in order to gain the time to do something you'd really rather do, great. All it takes is simple math— plus versus minus— to get there.

TIME SWAPPING EXAMPLE #1

We'll use a hobby as another example. Let's say you want to pursue a certain hobby. You figure, on average, you'll need to devote ten hours a week to it to start off. That's a little less than one and a half hours a day. Can you find one and a half hours' worth of roles to shift around in a day?

If you're committed to the hobby, the answer is yes, whether it's a little less sleep, a little less TV watching, a cutback in computer time, or a shift in your exercise schedule.

TIME SWAPPING EXAMPLE #2

If you have a specific goal in mind, such as writing a book or taking an online course, or building a tool shed, put that activity in your schedule. Set aside a regular amount of time every other day for this work. Doing this serves two purposes. First, you stop thinking that it's *something I'll get around to doing sometime*. Secondly, having the goal on the schedule makes it real, makes you more committed, and also helps give you the discipline to keep on task until the work is completed. If you have a regular appointment with that laptop or that table saw, you're more likely to follow through on your commitment.

You're simply reviewing where you spend your time and deciding whether to place that activity in a different area to get that flexibility you need. Over time, you will be able to settle into your various roles and see where you can borrow from them when new or unexpected roles pop up along the way.

TIME SWAPPING EXAMPLE #3

Then there are those times when there's a great shift in your schedule—times like vacations and holidays. Whether you have children or whether you have a spouse or a relationship you're involved in, you'll want to spend more time with them when your environment changes. How do you do that and still honor your other roles?

It's time to go back to that question: What are you willing to give in order to get the outcome you want? Do you show up at the family get-together grumpy, with your mind focused on all those things you told yourself you were going to do back home? Do you go to the holiday company party filled with resentment because you would really rather be home with your kids?

If you're going on vacation, ask yourself, "What do I want to experience this week?" Go back to the analogy of the movie theater. What movie script do I want to live today? Action? Adventure? Romance?

Comedy? Whatever you decide, mark time in your calendar. Make it real. Use juicy language to emphasize the emotional feelings you desire.

Let's say you want adventure on your vacation. Which roles honor adventure? You might conclude you need to improve your fitness because going on an adventure vacation could combine adventure and fitness at the same time. But in order to do that you would have to cut back in another area. You could make that happen. Then the following week you could go back to that norm that you have in a typical week.

TIME ISN'T THE PROBLEM TAKEAWAYS:

1. Here is the number of hours I think I need for the things I want to do. If the total is more than 168 hours, I can make these adjustments.
2. Here is one new activity that I would like to take on this week. This is how I can fit it into 168 hours.
3. I am willing to give this in order to achieve the outcome I desire.
4. I am not willing to give this in order to achieve the outcome I desire.

MAKE TIME WORK FOR YOU

"If you talk about it, it's a dream. If you envision it, it's exciting. If you plan for it, it's possible. If you schedule it, it's real."
—Tony Robbins

My dream is that everybody realizes that the time to live is now. I truly believe we all can, over time, transform ourselves from living lives of reaction, to living lives built on passion, creating lives that matter. That's what I am asking you to consider for yourself. Too many of us go through life stuck in that false believe that life is meant to be a struggle, and my mission is to show you that it doesn't have to be that way.

We all have items on our schedules, and a lot of information stuck in our head. My goal is for you to move from thought to action. Take one or two of those items in your head and write them down in your calendar. Now. Yes, stop reading and write them down NOW. By doing this, you are telling yourself that these items really matter to you and to the people you are doing them with.

I know that I'm a very ambitious person compared to most people. I am a planner at heart, and most people are not. If you are not a planner, you might be spurred to take action by asking yourself, "What would make a difference for me?" Then have the courage to commit to an amount of time to make this happen.

Becoming a planner, if you haven't been one as of yet, takes time and takes practice. I became committed to planning in my own life when I saw the results I reaped. I practiced planning until it became a habit, and now it feels natural and expected.

Right now, if you're like most people, what you have is a to-do list, if you have any list at all. We've already gone over why having that kind of list is futile and why the items on those lists tend to be avoided. It's the textbook example of living a life of reaction.

Now, let's take a look at what happens when you move from a to-do list to an actual schedule.

MAKE SCHEDULING A PRIORITY

To make the transition from a to-do list to a schedule, it's helpful to look at how business successes like Bill Gates, Warren Buffet, Oprah Winfrey, and Sir Richard Branson operate. I think everyone would agree that these people would be considered successful by society's standards. They seem to get an awful lot done and certainly live very full lives. But guess what? They live in the same 168-hour week as you do. How do they do manage their hours?

Answer: Prioritization. There is always going to be more to do in life than time to do everything you want. By prioritizing, you make sure that you get the important things done first. How do you make sure these things that you really want to happen get done in those 168 hours? Here's where we circle back to that all-important concept: Planning.

Everyone has dreams; everyone has those things they want to do—from everyday tasks or things on their bucket lists. But without planning, that's all they are, dreams. Disappointing dreams, too, as time passes and you're left with that empty feeling of nothing happening.

Are you convinced of the importance of planning and scheduling yet? I hope you are!

There's one other facet that also needs to be addressed in order to make a successful transition into being a person of action. That factor is balance. By finding and scheduling the time to do everything you want to do, you create the balance in your life you truly desire.

This starts with being present to what's going on in your life. Break down the roles you play in your life.

- How many hours a week do you want to devote to your important relationships?
- How many hours a week do you want to devote to your own personal development, which includes the physical, mental and spiritual?
- How many hours do you want to devote to your career?
- How many hours do you want to devote to your rest and recreation?
- How many hours do you want to devote to your community?

Right now you may have vague answers about all of these in your head. If that's where they stay, you may get lucky and get some of them done. But most likely you haven't sat down and realized that you've tried to cram 200 hours' worth of activities into those 168 hours.

Stop reading right now and get out a yellow pad or open a page on your laptop or tablet. Answer the questions posed here. Or for a more comprehensive, step-by-step approach, go through the process detailed at my website www.chadecooper.com. Then, when you're done, come back and read on to see how you can fit all of them into your life.

(Play the Jeopardy *Think Music* here while you take the time to answer these questions.)

THAT'S RIGHT, YOU REALLY NEED A SCHEDULE

I hate to sound like a CD player on repeat. But it's true. It all comes back to the schedule. A real schedule, not something that you plan out on a piece of paper that you then put on your desk or into a drawer and never see again. A real schedule that you can implement. A real schedule for your life.

In the next chapter, we're going to kick it up a notch, and show you how you can use this system to turn those dreams in your head into real, actionable items.

TIME ISN'T THE PROBLEM TAKEAWAYS:

Name three actions that you can take to move from the to-do list in your head to an actual calendar.

Create a schedule for the next week that you implement.

USE THIS TO TRANSFORM TIME

How do you go from, "I'm just trying to get through today" to "getting what I want, a life that matters"? Through your calendar you have two methods to do that. One is your schedule, which as you should realize by now, is a giant leap forward from the to-do list that's been gathering dust in your head. Having this written down, either on a computer or a paper planner, will move you into taking action, move you away from the life of reaction you've been stuck in up to this point.

This is great. Let's take a moment and recap the methods I've outlined to help you create a schedule that works for you:

Language - Descriptive words that use the visual, the auditory and the kinesthetic to inspire you to take action on your task.

Roles - Descriptive words that inspire you in all aspects of your life.

Color Coding - Assigning colors to the various roles of your life.

Balance - Determining the percentage of time you want to devote to particular items and managing this inside the 168-hour week.

Prioritization - Making the decisions on what is most important to you.

Purpose - Doing the inner work to determine your purpose in life and making a plan to put those plans into action.

Subject Line – Ensure that you use juicy language that reverts back to the strength in the purpose of the event itself. The Why.

Multitasking - Leverage your time by multitasking *when it makes sense.* For example, listening to an audio book while working out, or checking Facebook while watching television.

If you did nothing other than this, you'd be well on your way to a more streamlined life, and the likelihood of greater satisfaction at being able to be more efficient and more productive in your activities.

THE CAPTURE LIST [1]

Creating a schedule has its benefits. But there's one aspect a schedule can't address—the idea of adding new events into that already crowded 168-hour week. Sometimes, when faced with the prospect of taking on a new project, relationship, or activity, the tendency is to stop before starting. The pressure of not having enough time is daunting and feels heavy and onerous. The thought that sounded wonderfully appealing in your head gets shoved off to the side when the time comes to do something to make it happen.

However, there's a solution that can help get you off that stuck position. It's called The Capture List.

Unlike a to-do list, this type of list is a planning tool that helps you move those things that are not already on your schedule into your daily activities. The method shown here was developed by the training and consulting company, Mission Control (www.missioncontrol.com)

---

1 Mission Control Productivity, LLC Capture Tool referred as The Capture List

THE DOING NOW LIST

Here's the process. The Capture List is a series of lists. There are three levels. The first one is labeled *Doing Now.* This is the list that contains everything you're already doing in your life. Make this list your own. Start with whatever automatically pops in your head, even if it sounds silly or trivial to you. Have fun with this process. These are real things that you do. Things like:

- Buying milk.
- Writing a new resume.
- Needing golf balls for the match with the guys next week.
- Picking up a Valentine's card for your spouse.
- Seeing the dentist in two weeks.
- Sleeping in next Saturday morning.
- Building a deck on your house.
- Taking the kids to soccer practice this afternoon.
- Going to a concert next month.
- Finishing reading this book.

Just empty your head and write everything down. Often we think so far into the future that we aren't present with what we're doing now, and that's heavy, difficult, and exhausting.

Again, make this your own. There's a million different methods out there. Use the one that works for you, whatever that is, but have ONLY one. If you're old school, write down your list on a yellow pad or in a journal. I prefer technology. I happen to use Microsoft Outlook because this program seamlessly synchronizes to my phone, my tablet, and my computer. No matter where I am, if a thought comes to me, I can capture it and type it in or I can record and transcribe it into text.

Whatever method you use, it's important to be consistent. Don't create a computer list one day then put additional items on a paper list the next day. Stick to one location, and as those thoughts come in, you just throw them out on the *Doing Now* list.

Then pick a time **once a day** to devote to managing this list. Make this the same time every day, as this appointment with yourself is as important as anything else on your schedule. This should be as close as possible to what you consider the end of your day. However, at this point, your mission is to empty this list by putting it into your schedule.

Here's how you do this. Going back to the examples above, schedule that milk run either as a separate item or as something you could add to the grocery shopping trip that's already scheduled. If sleeping in on the weekend makes your list, make sure you've added an extra hour of sleep to your Saturday schedule. Same with the other items on the list. Move them from the *Doing Now* list to your schedule. If that means tomorrow, two weeks from now, two months from now, whatever that is, this goes on your schedule until either you have completely emptied your *Doing Now* list to your calendar and an empowering subject line event or cannot determine a date or time for it to currently fit onto your calendar.

THE NOT DOING NOW LIST

By the time you're done, the hope is that you're *Doing Now* list should be empty. If, however, you're like many people, there's bound to be something on the list that you haven't scheduled. Take the deck building in the list above. You might decide that even though it's something you want to do, it's going to take a little bit more thought than you have time for right now, and you truly don't know when you're going to do it… but you know you must get to it relatively soon within perhaps the next year or much sooner.

For items like this, there's a second list. This is called the *Not Doing Now* list. This list often includes those things that would most likely stay in your head as things you'll get around to *someday.* Having a list like this means that these items don't get forgotten, yet also recognizes the valid point that some ideas or projects need time to develop. You're giving yourself permission not to have to deal with this item right now.

How do you manage this list? Schedule about twenty minutes at the beginning of every week to devote to this list. Sunday mornings work best for me, but pick a time that works for you and stick with that time. It may take you less than twenty minutes to tackle, but you want to block out that amount of time. It's smarter to schedule more time for this list, especially when you're first starting out, than not enough. The goal is to make the management of these lists become a habit and then morph into a natural part of your life. If you don't schedule plenty of time for this at the beginning, this might take you longer than you expect to finish, and the frustration surrounding that might make you give up on the process prematurely. Remember, the idea is to win, and winning takes patience and persistence.

Here's a trick that helps keep you on track. Which is better: Allowing yourself more time than you think it's going to take and then end up being able to celebrate having ten minutes that you can put somewhere else? (Remember the beneficial joys of celebration?) Or, not enough time and going over? Padding extra time is a safer scenario than the one where you only give yourself ten minutes, discover that this takes more time, and wind up beating yourself up because you don't know where you're going to make up that time.

Now, take a detailed look at that *Not Doing Now* list. Take an item and calculate how many hours you anticipate needing for its completion. Using the example of building the deck, let's say you estimate it will take twenty hours to accomplish. That means you would need multiple appointments, multiple scheduled times. You could create twenty one hour blocks over the next several days or weeks or months, or four five hour blocks, or whatever way you want.

The point is to book this time out and schedule it, use empowering language to support yourself, use the role colors for enhancement, and have that commitment on your calendar.

Perhaps you have an even bigger project like a career change, making X amount of money to buy a specific item, or travel. Travel, for example, may encompass several things like researching where you want to go, finding the bargain deals, booking airfare, hotels, and the side excursions. Your first reaction might be that there's so much to do that you don't know where to begin. That feeling might stick with you without a method of how to plan.

Here's how to get this item into your *Doing Now* list. Start small. Schedule one hour in the coming week to start the process. Now you have the project on your calendar as a beginning. Then when you review you're *Not Doing Now* list the following week, you can repeat the action and schedule another hour to devote to the project, and keep doing that until the entire travel is planned out.

I used this method to create this book. I booked one hour on a Monday and a Friday every week to spend time creating this book. Now, if you know anything about writing, you'd realize that that's not a lot of time to devote to writing a book in a given week. That meant I needed a long time to get through this process. I could have gotten this done faster if I'd devoted more time each week to it. But those two hours a week was the maximum amount of time I had available, given all the other items on my schedule. Yes, the process was slower than I might have wanted. But *slower* was a much more productive and useful option than *never*.

The critical point is this. By using this method, the book got written. By placing this goal on my schedule and following through turned my dream of writing a book into a reality. If I had operated under the false belief that I needed lots of long stretches of time to write, this never would have happened.

Learning how to use the *Not Doing Now* list is a little like learning how to drive that stick shift. Admittedly, it's going to be awkward at first. Transitioning into a new system like this usually is. Give yourself ninety days. Here's why…

We're back to basic math again. The idea is to work on this list once a week at the beginning of every week. Ninety days works out to about twelve weeks. That means that I'm asking you to try to work on this list twelve times.

I can't make guarantees, but I'm willing to bet that by the twelfth time you're going to like the results.

THE DOING IN NEXT TWENTY YEARS LIST [2]

Now let's say you have a really big project. Maybe a bucket list item that right now may feel more like a wish than anything you see happening near term. You may have no idea where to begin. This is where the third and final capture list, the *Doing in the Next Twenty Years* list comes in.

Here's an example of how this list works. One of the dreams I have is to drive a Formula 1 racecar. I have no idea when I'm going to that. When the thought first came into my mind, I wrote it down in the *Not Doing Now* list. That next Sunday, when I realized I wasn't ready to commit to a day and time, I moved it into the *Doing in the Next Twenty Years* list. This goal was still a pipedream. I knew I wanted to drive a racecar someday, but didn't know when.

Therefore, I wasn't going to put in on my calendar. Instead, I gave myself permission to put this activity in the *Doing in the Next Twenty Years* folder. By creating this list, I have a place to put the items that have no date commitments. It's out of my head for now, but I haven't lost this

---

2 Mission Control Productivity, LLC Capture Tool Never Doing Now List (referred to as Doing In The Next Twenty Years)

goal entirely. Someday I plan on driving a Formula 1 racecar. When? Right now, it doesn't matter.

But by having this on my list, I will come back to it at another time. I'm acknowledging that there's more to do in life than I will have time to do, but I don't want to forget this. Maybe somewhere down the road I might find a space to turn this interest into a reality.

Every ninety days, I put an appointment on my schedule to devote thirty minutes to review the *Doing in the Next Twenty Years* list. I picked ninety days because this time interval works for me, but you can make this as short or as long as you want. When you look at this list, you ask yourself, *what dream do I want to begin making real*?"

Most of the time you're likely to say you're not ready, and keep the activity on the list. But there will come a time when inspiration will hit, and you will be able to see how you could plan over this amount of weeks or that amount of time to make this interest happen. At that point, you start to schedule time on your calendar, in order to put your plan into action.

For example, I'd wanted to learn how to speak Russian for the longest time, but this desire stayed on my long-term list because I didn't see a reason why I should make room for it on my active list. I then got involved in a project to help the children from the Chernobyl fallout zone. Now I had a real reason to learn Russian! I was motivated to move this to my *Doing Now* list.

How did I make this happen? I did two things. First, I identified when I needed to be complete in the objective and marked this finish point of celebration on my calendar. Next, I then worked backwards from that date and determined how much time each week I likely would need to devote to the "Why" of this goal. I then scheduled forty minutes on my calendar for language lessons every week. Being very purposeful, I multitasked by arranging to do this while working out. Then having these Russian children as houseguests reinforced this new skill, and by the end of their trip I was speaking Russian fluently. (At least fluently by American standards.)

There's another reason for putting your wish list items on this long-term list. Something that may seem "pie in the sky" right now might become more realistic a few years down the road. For example, for those too young to remember, when cell phones first came out they were very expensive and the average person most likely believed they would always be out of reach. This could have been on somebody's *Doing in the Next Twenty Years* list. As prices came down, not only was it possible but also likely to see a purchase like this happening, enabling *buying a cell phone* to be moved to the *Doing Now* list.

One of the items that's been on my *Doing in the Next Twenty Years* list is going up in space. A few years ago, I would have been content to keep this as a lovely daydream, as I believed I'd never become an astronaut in this lifetime.

But now private companies have started to spring up, offering rides in space to civilians. Granted, right now it's very expensive, and they're still only available on a limited basis. In the coming years, however, as they perfect the rockets and their business models, the prices are likely to come down somewhat. True, space travel will probably always be pricey, but I'm now able to entertain the possibility that this can really happen for me. It's still on my list, and I still have the opportunity to evaluate, and make my decision accordingly.

USING THE CAPTURE LIST FOR RETIREMENT

Surveys reveal that too many people have not planned properly for retirement. In one survey of people 50-65, only forty-seven percent—that's less than half—had concrete written goals on how they would prepare for retirement. In most cases, all this meant was that they'd met with a financial planner and developed a monetary retirement plan.

But the number of survey respondents who went on to say that they knew what they were going to do in retirement dropped down to a measly thirty-seven percent. To me that's a scary statistic. Over six out of ten people go off into retirement with nothing to do and no goals in mind. Another seven out of ten people don't even know when they're going to retire. They've got a plan but they don't have a date set.

By now, you ought to know what happens if you leave your plans in your head. The people who haven't planned financially for retirement might end up having to work for the rest of their lives out of necessity, or scale back their lifestyles dramatically if their only source of income is coming from Social Security. The ones who do have the money to retire but no plans, will find themselves bored and either go back to work to maintain an identity and feel needed, or fill their days with unhealthy behaviors so they achieve significance or feel connected to others. Those who plan to retire "someday" may come to see that someday will never come.

If you want to plan effectively for retirement activities, write down your goals and put them on the *Doing in the Next Twenty Years* list. Then every ninety days, take out the list and ask these questions:

- Am I ready for this?
- How do I become ready?
- What do I want to become?

Don't feel pressure that you have to follow through. Give yourself permission to say, "Maybe I'll never do this thing, and it's likely I won't."

MASTERING YOUR BUCKET LIST

In 2007, *The Bucket List*, starring Jack Nicholson and Morgan Freeman, premiered in theaters worldwide. Nicholson and Freeman play two terminally-ill cancer patients who decide to set out on a road trip and do all the things they really want to do before they die—in other words, their bucket lists.

The *Doing in the Next Twenty Years* list is the ultimate bucket list. Remember how I mentioned how many bucket list items I've been able to do? This is how I did them. I just wrote down every crazy idea I could think of. The process of having them written down afforded me the opportunity to look at them, evaluate them, and realize that with planning and resourcefulness I could make them happen.

One day I gathered together the various lists I created over the years and started checking off what I'd accomplished. Reviewing my bucket list was a real eye-opener. I was still in my late thirties, and to my surprise and amazement I'd *already* done 900 of the 1,000 most popular bucket list items. In truth, I'd achieved more than what was on *most* people's bucket lists. This eventually led me to apply for a Guinness Book of World Record Holder, as the person with the longest list of accomplished bucket-list items. This was an item I at one point had previously put on my *Doing in the Next Twenty* Years capture list. All of which has led to the next bullet point in my bucket list: this book.

I still have other wild ideas on my list. Owning a World War II fighter plane, for one. I don't even know how to fly yet. Guess what? I don't have to. I don't ever have to. At some point though, if I decide I'm ready to own a World War II plane then I can start by putting *get a pilot license* in my calendar. I can schedule out a couple of days or weeks to go get my pilot's license. I can then work on the next piece and the next piece. But if I look at the whole thing as all encompassing, I'll never start.

TIME ISN'T THE PROBLEM TAKEAWAYS:

1. For the next week, work on your *Doing Now* list. Whatever you can't schedule each day, put in your *Not Doing N*ow list.

2. These are the items I can move up to my calendar at the beginning of each week.
3. This is how I can incorporate my retirement plans into these lists.

YOUR BIGGEST TIME WASTER

If you only have 168 hours in a week are you being purposeful with that time?

When you are purposeful, you start being the source of your own experience rather than being the default of other people's experiences. If you don't live by your standard, other people are going to put their standards on you, and you probably won't like them.

Be deliberate. Your time is *your* time. Choose best how your schedule will service you.

Unfortunately, because we live in a technological world, your best-laid plans could be undone by one of the biggest time wasters around these days.

Email.

The number two problem that people ages 50-65 complain about is having to constantly monitor or being absorbed in their e-mail. Like mice in a maze, they feel compelled to stop whatever they're doing when they hear that ding that lets them know they've got a new message.

It doesn't have to be this way. If you do nothing else, stop living by your e-mail. This decision will enhance your life. Turn off the audible notification of e-mail coming in on all your devices—your phone, desktop, laptop, or tablet.

Seriously, DO IT. NOW.

I learned this valuable lesson back when I was still working in the IT Industry. On average I got about 300-350 e-mails a day, with that annoying "ding-ding-ding-ding-ding" going through my body, sounding like nails on a chalkboard. This stressed me out and I had to get rid of that awful chime just to save my sanity.

Let's face facts. An email list is like a task list in a different format, but it's a task list nevertheless—lots of people either wanting things from you, responding to things you want from them, or just people trying to sell you something. (We won't even get into spam here.) What's that email task list doing? It's getting bigger and bigger and never ending.

Here's where your schedule comes into play. Instead of relying on those dings as your prompts, schedule time to go over your email. Decide what time intervals work best for you and stick to them. If you get 350 emails a day, it's going to take you a little bit more time than somebody who gets twenty a day. I find that three times a day works for me, but I'm not going to hold you to that. Work out a plan that honors your needs and requirements.

Then make sure this time is devoted solely to email processing. Don't try to multitask by saying you'll check email when you're with your spouse or doing hobbies. The likelihood is that email will take over because that's what you've been trained to do. You will sacrifice your own personal needs to be a slave to those electronic commands.

Important note: When you change your email reading habit, make sure you let everyone know. Chances are, your contacts have grown accustomed to getting instant responses from you, and you don't want them to feel as if you've ignored or abandoned them. Send them an email that says something to the effect of, "In order to serve you, I want to make sure that I have quality time to focus on your needs. Therefore, I will be checking my email three times a day." Then add this note to your signature address in case they missed your message the first time. "I just want to let you know e-mail is a great form of communication. I check e-mail three times a day. If you have something that's urgent, please mark it as urgent and text me or give me a call." Let your contacts know how to play by your rules and help set them up to win.

THE TWO-MINUTE RULE

Once you've gotten yourself on an email schedule, then it's time to apply the capture list to these daily messages. At the end of the day, or the last time of the day you check your email, empty your inbox. That's right, I said *empty your inbox*. Leave no unopened mail in there.

Sound impossible? Not really. Here's how to do it. Look at each item. If it's going to take you less than two minutes to respond to the email, respond to it. Then either delete it or put it in the folder you designate for completed emails. If it will take you longer than two minutes to react to it, then move the item into your *Doing Now* bin or put it on your calendar. If you conclude the email is not a high priority, then put it in the *Not Doing Now* list. The point is that everything gets moved, and nothing gets left in your inbox.

WHILE WE'RE ON THE SUBJECT...

Facebook and Twitter and Instagram – let's just call them social media—are great tools, used in the right context, in the right time, and in the right quantity.

But because it's not scheduled, your time spent on social media can get out of control. This makes you more likely to become addicted and absorbed. The minute you planned to check your friend's post becomes a rabbit hole of birthdays, cat pictures, inspirational sayings, and the latest viral video, and the next thing you know, it's a half an hour later.

Again, here's where scheduling comes in. Block out a set period of time—five minutes, ten minutes, whatever—for your attention to social media. Be deliberate with that time. Put *checking social media* in your schedule for a specific amount of time. You may even want to set an alarm, especially if you've been using Facebook browsing as an excuse to procrastinate. You can also tell yourself, "Maybe I need to have some parameters to earn this as a treat."

If you find yourself in a position where you want to spend more time online, ask yourself, "What am I gaining from doing this? Is this a distraction or serving me in some capacity in either in my own life or in service to other people?" If the answer is the former, then perhaps it's a personal hobby and you want to schedule that time accordingly and label it with the juicy language you use for personal pursuits.

Often, people flock to Facebook for connection, to see what their friends are doing, to look up old acquaintances from the past. There is nothing wrong with that. But as with all aspects of your life, make this time purposeful. Schedule this appointment, using the language that supports the experience you want. If your goal is connection, put in the subject line, *connecting with old friends* or something to that effect. Don't just put *Facebook time.*

TIME ISN'T THE PROBLEM TAKEAWAYS:

1. Make a schedule for email checking that works for you. How does this differ from what you're doing now? This is how this new schedule differs from what I am doing now.
2. Make a schedule for time spent on social media. How does this differ from what you're doing now? This is how this new schedule differs from what I am doing now.

GOOD NEWS FOR THOSE WHO HAVE STUCK AROUND TO THIS POINT

Now that we're on the road to transform stress into success, let's take a moment and reiterate some important points.

- Start your day with intention. Start your day deliberate. Look at your schedule and say, "Is there anything here that needs to be adjusted?" If so, take action and reschedule that activity. Decide how much time to dedicate to the role, describe it in fun and empowering language, and assign a color.
- If you're working with individual items, put in the colors that represent that role to enhance it. Use language that supports and empowers you, to make the activity an experience you honor, anticipate, and find rewarding.

Anytime that I can put an experience on my calendar that honors more than myself, that's the fuel in life. That's where things really get juicy. That's where life starts to matter. If George W. Bush can make up words, I can too. I say you should have a ***strategery***. By this, I mean that you should have enough self-confidence that you don't care if people are going to judge or criticize you for the words and creativity that you have abundant inside of you. If you're able to use your *strategery* to lead to an extraordinary life, that's really all that matters. Your confidence in yourself and the ability to execute on that is going to make people turns their heads and find both you and your beliefs inspiring.

This kind of confidence is why real estate agents will plaster bus benches with loud and seemingly obnoxious colors and words. They are meant to grab your attention. The point is not to be afraid to stand out vs. conform. Have fun with it. People who act out of the box and stand out are noticed. Sometimes that's exactly what we need to do to take action.

For me to have a life that matters, I had to create a list of things that were important to me. Foremost on that list was the desire to spend more time with my spouse and to have a career change, which in my case meant being able to retire from the corporate world to do whatever I wanted. There was a lot at stake, as I've mentioned earlier. At first I believed I couldn't afford to walk away, and that could have stopped me in my tracks if I held on to that belief.

So, how did I get from "this is no longer becoming fun" to taking steps and finally exiting that world? The first component was identity. I had to have the courage to take a hard look at myself, my attributes and my abilities.

Who was I? I was well-educated and significant. I was needed, making a difference and could really do my job well. I was successful. As Nike says, I'm the type of guy who believes "just do it".

Part of figuring out my identity was also answering the question: Am I this job? Was I so wrapped up in what I did that I couldn't afford to take the risk to exit? Would I have to re-skill myself? In this phase of thought I came face-to-face with fear—False Emotions Appearing Real—versus danger.

To get beyond that fear, I had to stay focused. I got there by believing my goals were bigger than these false emotions appearing real. What I did holds true for anyone looking to break away from any restricting beliefs. This brings us back to identity; knowing who you are and having a goal and vision down the road.

At first, there's a big gap between your vision and the result you desire. The first step toward getting that result is actually visualizing that goal. Think about it. This really isn't a new idea for you. Remember back to when you were a kid and the whole world was open to you? Back then you believed you could be anything you wanted to be. Then somewhere along the way you got trained to be "realistic". If you're like most people, your trajectory probably went something like this:

YOU SAID	YOU WERE TOLD
I want to be an astronaut.	That's impossible.
I want to get into a top university.	You'll never have the grades to get in.
I want to get a great job.	In this economy, you're lucky to get what you have.
I want to get promoted.	You're not good enough.
I want to go on my dream vacation.	You're lucky to pay your bills, stop day dreaming.
I really want this fancy car.	You need to keep working to feed your family and not focusing on wasting money you don't have.

I'm going to give you the opportunity now to look at this from a different perspective. I can't take away anything that's happened in the past, but what if, starting now, you brought your thinking back to the endless possibilities you saw as a kid? If you had no limitations—money, travel, family was no object— what would you want to do?

I'll bet at least a few things come to mind. Now that you've learned how to move beyond fear and how to plan and schedule these things in a way that instills passion and persistence, you're ready to begin!

TIME ISN'T THE PROBLEM TAKEAWAYS:

1. I dreamed of becoming this when I was a kid. If I didn't achieve it, this is why.
2. This is what I want to achieve now. This is what is holding me back.
3. I am willing to give this in return for the outcome I desire. I am willing to fully commit to these methods to may my dream a reality.

ROME WASN'T BUILT IN A DAY—NEITHER WAS YOUR SCHEDULE

Now that I've got you convinced of the benefits of planning and scheduling, I'm going to add one more thing.

Relax.

You're not going to sit down and say, "I'm going to schedule out my next year" —or the next three years for that matter. Most people don't have the desire or the habits to do that. If that's what you think this is all about, then you're most likely never to start at all.

I'll admit planning can be a daunting task. If you're ambitious, creative, or even a little crazy, you might end up with a capture list with 500 items on it. It's enough to give anyone pause. Therefore, this is the time to take a deep breath and remind yourself that you don't need to create a full-blown schedule all at once. Start with your *Doing Now* capture list and put one item into your schedule. Then two, then three. Then next week, give yourself twenty minutes or half hour to look over those *Not Doing Now* items. If you can't see where they fit, don't feel pressured to be perfect. Do what you can and simply schedule another event to complete it later. We are not seeking perfection, rather positive habits. As the practice of scheduling becomes more familiar to you, you'll feel the urge to add and balance. You might even turn this into a game and give yourself a reward every time you move an item out of your capture list and into your schedule.

The question arises, what do you do when you find yourself needing to add something to your schedule that you really don't want to do, like an obligation that's more of a duty than a desire? Maybe something unpleasant that you've been avoiding, but know deep down is something you really have to do.

Start with language. Find a way to reframe this task to make it less onerous. For example, if you're a boss and you have to fire somebody, don't put *fire X* on your schedule. Reframe this as *giving X new opportunities.* Or if you need to schedule a colonoscopy, write down *taking positive action to insure my good health.*

It's all in the way you look at things. For example, I can ask somebody, "What is your favorite food?"

"Pizza," he says.

"Great. If I could give you pizza tomorrow, would you like it?"

"Yes, that would be great."

"Now if that's all you could eat, how would you feel?

"That's all I can eat?"

"That's right. Pizza three times a day, every day for the rest of your life."

All of a sudden that delicious pizza becomes an ugly, steamy pile of stuff.

Put your intentions, your missions, your tasks in the best possible light, and you're more likely to see them through to fruition. "Just for today, I am going to enjoy the tasty satisfying flavor of pizza."

TIME ISN'T THE PROBLEM TAKEAWAYS:

1. This is how I deal with unpleasant tasks.
2. This is how I can change the language of an unpleasant task to make it more palatable. (Ensure there is a strong WHY associated to the task and the meaning changes from a "have to" to a "get to" experience.)

PADDING—IT'S NOT JUST FOR FURNITURE

What about the unexpected? What happens when something unplanned comes up that really can throw your schedule off kilter? Does this plan go out the window?

No.

In fact, my wife and I have a running joke. "You schedule when you're going to be spontaneous, don't you?" she says.

I laugh back and say, "Yes, I do."

Scheduled spontaneity may sound like an oxymoron. It's not. It's about being fluid and cultivating an attitude that welcomes possibilities and doesn't dread them. It's the difference between telling yourself, "These are the things I would like to experience today", and saying, "These are a bunch of things I must get done today or else."

Now, on the surface, there's nothing wrong with the latter. A lot of people get by fine by holding to a rigid structure in their lives. This works well as long as nothing else gets in the way. When you force yourself into a rigid structure scheduled things can get done in the preferred order, tasks accomplished.

However, being rigid and holding on to a set way of being has one drawback. This doesn't allow for the unforeseen. This doesn't leave room for the unexpected. Without flexibility, you could be left in the position of having to move things around or, even worse, not accomplishing the things you really want to do, just to take care of something you *have* to do.

One way to deal with this situation is to add something else to the schedule. I call this *padding*. It's a way of creating space, of giving yourself enough flexibility and time capability to handle whatever new items come into play. Having this extra space allows you the freedom to take care of that particular situation along with the tasks or items that are already on your agenda.

How would that work in everyday scenarios? Let's say a friend calls up and wants to get together. You already have a busy schedule for the day. But since you have allowed for padding, you have the ability to create the space to spend time with your friend. If it's something that's important and matters to you, you've scheduled time to do that.

Inevitably, emergencies are going to happen. By scheduling padding into your daily life, you have the space to take care of anything unusual that pops up without getting stressed out. You avoid the situation of punishing yourself for being so rigid that you can't embrace the unexpected experiences that might arise.

But there's another situation to consider. When is an emergency a "real emergency"? Why did this situation become urgent in the first place? Often this happens because we didn't deal with the item previously, when it could have been handled without that feeling of urgency. This is a fancy way of saying *procrastination*.

Some people manage to use procrastination to their advantage. For them it's a motivating tool. The pressures of waiting till the last minute to get something done becomes the impetus that's needed for getting the item accomplished. They used that urgency as a tool to take action.

Unfortunately, this often doesn't work, especially if some other emergency comes up that gets in the way of the emergency that has to be dealt with, because the action to take care of it in the first place was put off. This creates stress. If it's a chronic situation, the stress will mount up and possibly lead to a total meltdown.

No one wants that. But there is a way out. There are various tools available for keeping your tasks in an orderly flow. My preferred method is writing everything down, enabling you to have a hard copy of the items in front of you. That visual cue helps to organize activities to allow for the padding that will keep things moving smoothly.

There are several ways to go about this. You can physically write it down. My foolproof solution is to record into my phone. These days most everybody has this capability; anyone can hit the record button and memorialize their thoughts. As it's portable, this gives you the opportunity to record anywhere, whether you're driving, sitting behind a desk or even in bed. The flow exists because your mind works faster than what you can type or what you can write. To honor that is to create the space.

The important thing is to get your thoughts out. Once it's recorded you can replay them and either write down the critical course of action or deal with it immediately in that moment.

Here's another way of looking at it. Go back to that movie theater story of your life. Would your show be a blockbuster that people would like to see like *Adventures In communication 101 with the credit card company*? Or would it be a bomb called *Must get the thieving credit card company to remove bogus charges*? Which one would you rather see? Which one would you rather create?

For the script of your life to be a blockbuster, you need to create space for unexpected events. Room for spontaneity. Space to honor when you need to recharge, when you need to take a break or when you need to allow something to come out.

I often equate this way of thinking to putting a beet on a salad. What happens when you put a beet on a salad? The juice bleeds out to the rest of the salad. In that same way, creating space will bleed out into all of the other roles that you have in life. It becomes very addictive and very supporting to say, "This is a choice. I get to choose what this means. I choose to make this an experience that's fun, that's inviting, that's joyful, that is enthusiastic, and I'm creating enough space to do it."

TIME ISN'T THE PROBLEM TAKEAWAYS:

1. I have a full schedule. Suddenly I get a phone call from an old friend who's in town for today only. I really want to see this friend. These are the three scenarios that I can use to make this work and still meet my other obligations.

WANNA LIVE HAPPILY EVER AFTER?

Mission Control calls the *Doing in the Next Twenty Years* list the *Not Doing Never List.* My reworking of this label was inspired by one of my clients who was seventy-two years old and had a bucket list for the next thirty years.

My first reaction was to want to shout out, "Wait a minute. You're not going to live to 103. Don't you think thirty years is unrealistic? Maybe you should dial that back to five. After all, you shouldn't be buying a dozen bananas either at this point."

Fortunately, I didn't say those things aloud. I caught myself, as I realized the limiting beliefs I had about age and activity. I meant well, but that kind of language has the intent of telling someone, "Maybe I shouldn't dream. You're right; I guess I won't make that happen."

Don't let any limiting beliefs you might have get in the way of your bucket list. Give yourself permission to put anything on that list that you can think of. If this week goes by or that timeframe goes by, and you tell yourself, "I'm not ready to deal with this," it's okay. Just let it be. Don't feel as if you need to make a decision then and there. There's a saying "walk as far as you can see, and when you get there you can see further." Kick your bucket down as far as you can see, when you get there your dream will still be there for you.

Admittedly, finding a way to start working on a dream can be hard for some. That's why it's very important to have a community. I'm a firm believer in groups and in finding time to be with others who will support the outcomes you want. They can be your accountability partners.

Find your buddies and work on your capture lists as a group. Make plans to get together over a meal every ninety days. Make an event of it. Be diligent with your time. Spend an hour together figuring out how you can pick one item off your list and put it in your calendar. Hooray! By doing this, you've taken another step toward action.

Another option is to join a Mastermind. The difference there is that you must have something to contribute or you get kicked out. Second, if you don't follow through with your commitments, you get kicked out, period. You cannot escape and say, "I'm going to give you a really compelling story about why I didn't do anything." They'll go, "Great, you're out." You have to follow up on what you're saying you're going to do by taking action.

I also firmly believe in what I call the rat pack theory. In order for a marriage to be passionate, I believe that both spouses need time with their like gender. Men get away and go spend time with other guys, while women go spend time with other women. My wife and I both subscribe to this philosophy. She goes off and has her weekends. I go off and I go do manly things with the guys.

That's also an opportunity to sit down and say, "Guys, how do we want to make our wives feel special?" I don't pretend to have all the right answers. What I do is surround myself with wise people who shore up my weaknesses, people who can say, "Have you thought about this?" I could answer, "No, I didn't. That would be perfect I could do that."

Being around like-minded people can also give you the encouragement that's going to help you follow through. Start with the ninety minute meetings. By the way, if you do that just four times a year, imagine where your life is going to be a year from now.

That alone, over time, three years from now, will project you into a very different experience in life from where you are today. Imagine if you just took a little bit of action on your finances persistently over ninety days at a time what that would do three years from now? What that would do twenty years from now?

It's not about saying, "I have to do everything right now." It's about breaking down the 168 hours and saying this week I'm going to give a little bit more attention to this role and a little less attention to this role.

TIME ISN'T THE PROBLEM TAKEAWAYS:

1. Create an accountability partner or group. Make firm plans to meet.
2. This is one item I can discuss with the group.
3. We will hold each other to these standards.

ANOTHER THING THAT'S WRONG WITH THE TO DO LIST

"It's not your strength that holds you to your purpose, it's the strength of your purpose itself."

—Al Granum

Why use a schedule-based solution or system over a to-do list? First and foremost, a to-do list continues to build and get longer. By design, you're compelled to look at the entire thing. A schedule however gives you the luxury and the choice of saying, "How much do I want to look at?" Typically, I'll look first at a day and then at the entire week. That way, I get a big picture, and a snapshot.

Here's the benefit in that. The colors that I use in my schedule really stand out when looked at over a week's time. Those colors represent roles that I'm going to act out on the stage of life for both the day and the week. What's nice about this is I can narrow that view just for today. Yesterday goes off the list, unless I deliberately choose to pick up yesterday in order to celebrate my successes.

With a task list, however, even if you check things off, you're still seeing this all-encompassing, monumental, stress-building list that can't help but wear you out. I mean, it's heavy to carry that sucker around.

The schedule is going to be structured in a linear way that sets out the priorities of the day. You can move things around to make the day play out in the way you desire. You could say, "If I want action, I simply move everything off that's not action." You can't do that with a to-do list.

A schedule allows you to be very dynamic. If there's a different priority that comes in for the day, something that's urgent and important, you have the ability to quickly move that around. Schedules also give you the ability to write in the strength of the purpose. A to-do list also is part of your massive action, but to-dos rarely include the purpose themselves.

With the growth of smart phones, has come the growth of apps. There are some out there that can help you with motivation, give you inspiration, and help you do things repeatedly to set up your day on the right foot. Remember, a bad beginning makes for a bad ending. A great beginning, however, makes for a great ending.

I'll share what I'm using right now, because it's working for me now. But because technologies come and go so quickly, there may even be a more evolved method out there by the time this book is released.

I use a free tool called Mindbloom. You can download this app from the web for your smart phone. It's an accountability tool that's configured as a little tree, and each leaf represents the different roles in your life. What I love about Mindbloom is I can put things on there that are motivating. Another great feature is its ability to bring up a new inspirational quote each day.

This app is also helpful if you're in a position where you don't have a huge support group around you. It can serve as a virtual support group by indicating that if you aren't taking action on these items, the leaf turns from green to yellow to brown. You have to continue to nourish the tree at the roots to keep it full and blossoming.

The app also gives you the ability to program in simple things. As an example, if I want to be a more caring husband, I have a message that comes up and says, "Say I love you."

For a guy, that might be critical. This may not be your default habit if you were raised in a house where those emotions weren't openly expressed. But guess what? This might be your spouses', and that's what she needs.

TIME ISN'T THE PROBLEM TAKEAWAYS:

1. Name three benefits of the schedule over the to-do list.
2. This is what would motivate me to stick to this schedule.

WHAT ROCKS HAVE TO DO WITH YOUR SUCCESS

When I first started studying time management, I was naturally drawn to the concepts and approaches championed by such time management gurus as Steven Covey and Ken Blanchard. One of Covey's analogies that really resonated with me was the story of the glass and rocks. Covey would stand in front of a group, put a bunch of stones into an empty glass and then ask, "Is the glass full?"

The audience would respond, "Yes, of course it's full."

Then Covey would pour a bag of smaller rocks into the glass, filling in the gaps between the larger ones. "Now, is the glass full?" he would ask.

"Well, yes it's full," the audience replied.

Finally, he'd take out a bag of sand and pour it into the glass until all the gaps were filled.

How does this relate to your schedule? Your schedule is as full as you perceive it to be.

Full is a matter of perception.

Mike Schmidt, the CEO of Nike, performed the same glass and rocks demonstration with a group of students. But his conclusion was different. After he put in the sand, he poured a pitcher of water into the glass.

Then he looked at the class and asked, "What's the point of this illustration?"

One eager beaver raised his hand and said, "The point is no matter how full your schedule is, if you try really hard you can always fit some more things into it."

Now that's what most of us would think. But Mike Schmidt replied, "No. That's not the point. **The truth is, if you don't put the big rocks in first you will never get them in. The big stones represent the most important things. They need to be addressed first**, before you fill in the gaps with things to utilize but aren't as important."

What are the big rocks in your life? Are you putting them first? Things like time with your loved ones, your spiritual time, your education, your dreams, worthy causes, teaching or mentoring others. Remember to put these big rocks in first or you'll never get them all in.

Covey also developed a matrix with four quadrants in it that helps visualize this concept. He breaks out items into these four categories:

- Important and not urgent - in the upper left-hand quadrant
- Not important and urgent - in the lower left-hand quadrant
- Important and urgent - in the upper right-hand quadrant
- Not important and not urgent - in the lower right-hand quadrant

COVEY'S MATRIX

IMPORTANT AND NOT URGENT	IMPORTANT AND URGENT
NOT IMPROTANT AND URGENT	NOT IMPORTANT AND NOT URGENT

Where should you be spending the bulk of your time? Procrastinators would say you spend the bulk of your time in the important and urgent area because they procrastinated and they're working under the pressure of "it's urgent and important that I get it done or I'm really going to fail." They use that as leverage to get them to take action. But that also takes a lot of energy and loss of momentum in the process. To go from 0 to 100 burns a lot of fuel.

To make the most efficient use of your time and energy you want to operate from the important but not urgent quadrant.

Plan, be decisive, prioritize and say, "This is what's most important and then the next most important comes in, and then after that I fill that time in." Tony Robbins, as an example, came up with the term of NET time, No Extra Time. That's where you can do important stuff like exercise, take care your health, and your education while doing something else like a daily drive commute. These are examples of things that are important and not urgent.

One way to make the biggest impact on your day is to reduce or eliminate items that are not important and not urgent. For some, email, Facebook, Twitter, or television fall into this category. Or make those activities purposeful by multitasking with something important and not urgent, such as reading or working out or housework. Use juicy, exciting, and empowering words to represent the roles that you want to play out today. Spice up your appointments with dynamic and powerful language that helps keep you enthusiastic, passionate, and committed to the task at hand.

TIME ISN'T THE PROBLEM TAKEAWAYS:

1. Name two activities in your current schedule that fit into each of the four quadrants.
2. These activities can be reworked to fit into the important and not urgent category.
3. Create time on your calendar to complete this activity.

MORE ON WHY YOU DO WHAT YOU DO

Why are you doing the things that you don't want to do, the things that you say you don't want to do but you do anyway, and then you have things that you say you want to do, but yet you aren't taking action on those. It's really very elementary.

Go on. Admit it. You like this feeling.

You do the things that you say you don't want to do, because at the time they fulfill an emotional need. You even tell yourself you feel fine, even if deep down, you honestly know these things are not right for you. What you're really doing is satisfying a need to connect with yourself. You're doing something that feels satisfying in the moment, because of something that happened earlier that day or that week that you didn't like. You want to get rid of that sad or lonely feeling.

A lot of the time these things we do aren't healthy for us, like binging on fast food when we're trying to lose weight. Or they're unproductive uses of time, like watching too much television or spending too much time surfing the internet. While these actions allow us to connect, it's a shallow, fleeting connection that doesn't really benefit us long term. This doesn't serve the greater good.

What's the alternative?

Truth is you already know the answers. Eat healthier. Exercise. Save money. Spend more time with the ones you love. Sometimes, though, the amount of work to get there seems like a really uphill battle. You might look at the situation and say, "Yes once I'm there the result would be really valuable for me. But man, donuts really sound tasty right now. I'll just have one or six."

If you're doing something that you don't want to do but you're doing anyway, look at how it's meeting your needs. Look at how it's fulfilling you. Are you getting connection? Does it make you feel important, wanted, and needed? You might feel something good in that moment. But does that feeling come at the expenses of your long term goals?

The next time you're tempted to procrastinate or take the easy way out, ask yourself this. "How will this purchase, this decision, or this item improve my life?" If the answer is, "In the moment great, but long term I need to come up with some powerful solutions," then you know it's not the right choice to make. It would be more productive to spend your time elsewhere.

To have a life that matters, you will want to focus your time and attention on things that will bring you security and comfort for brief durations, but in reality great lives happen when we add growth and variety. You've hear the phrase "variety is the spice of life", well without it you have bland and boring. Yes, comfort is wonderful, but like the previous comment about eating pizza every meal forever, you get tired of it. So, schedule things that allow you to feel connected and have a relationship with somebody. Then, using this system will allow you to get past those times when you'd rather procrastinate because it automatically insert both certainty and spice, which will enable you to build the bridge to your goals that is purposeful but enjoyable at the same time.

Once you embrace a schedule based planning system, really make it your own. If you're using pen and paper, buy yourself the nicest journal you can find. Bookstores, office supply stores, paper stores—both brick and mortar and on the internet—have lots of varieties of paper-based scheduling systems. Pick out an attractive, hardbound binder that you can feel really proud about carrying. By keeping everything in one system, you're able to go back over time and look at the things you've accomplished, celebrate those victories, and remember the skills that you've learned.

I'm a realist and am aware that shifting into a new system is going to have its ups and downs, and there are going to be times when you might get so frustrated that you're tempted to throw the whole thing out. Those are the times when you're going to want to review where you've been, and see that this system has worked for you and allow you to recognize the victories both small and even some big. This will remind you of where you started and show you visible proof of how far you've come. It's sort of the equivalent of a pat on the back and could be just the encouragement you need to get you past your momentary slump.

This will be especially true if you take into account the VAK. Use colored pens, highlighters, or pencils to add that visual appeal. Write in that color or highlight in that color that represents the role of the experience you want to have. The same can be done electronically on your computer based planner.

Don't forget your language. Be creative with the juicy words you use to excite yourself. If you measured the energy of your words on a scale of 0 to 10, make sure they're all 10s or at minimum 7.5. Instead of getting a haircut, consider *getting my mojo back by looking good.* Writing a business report? How about *creatively making my company grow richer?* Cooking dinner can become *keeping my family healthy.* Tie your words to the experience that you want to have. Don't make the task a chore, or an arduous, heavy *have to do.* Instead, go with something like *I get to do this and get something beneficial in return.*

Structure your day in a way that allows you to win. Schedule in five to ten minutes a day to focus on being present. Make sure you're aware of where your priorities lie and that they're in your schedule. If there's something that you're hesitant about doing, use empowering language that encourages you to stay focused and see your goal to completion. Everything else after that will be a celebration. You'll be able to say, "I got to do this because I got the important stuff done first."

PARETO'S PRINCIPLE

How do you move from being active to being productive in your life? Something to consider here is the concept known as Pareto's Principle. Also known as the 80/20 rule, and used primarily in business, Pareto's Principle states that roughly eighty percent of the effects of something are due to twenty percent of the causes. In business, for example, this means that eighty percent of profits come from twenty percent of the clients. In the computer world, eighty percent of the bugs in software come from twenty percent of the code.

You can apply Pareto's Principle to your scheduling system. When you first start out, focus on the twenty percent that matters the most and put aside the other eighty percent for now. That twenty percent will move you forward, and will have an impact. Make that twenty percent count. Focus on what's important, not the fluff. Then when you have time and you're more comfortable with the concept, bring the other eighty percent in.

TIME ISN'T THE PROBLEM TAKEAWAYS:

1. I react in this way when I'm tempted by distractions.
2. I can prevent being tempted by distractions in the future by changing the language and strengthen the purpose in this way.

NOW YOU'RE COOKING

"Life goes by pretty quick, if you don't stop and take a look around, you might just miss it."

—Ferris Bueller's Day Off

Congratulations. You've come a long way. You've come to see the value of this system. Perhaps you've even started to use some of these principles. Hint: If you've been answering the questions and practicing the end of the chapter takeaways up to this point, you already are!

Once you start using the system, people around you will notice. They'll see you keeping your appointments, staying on schedule, perhaps paying more attention to them than you have previously. Maybe you've even appointed one of them as your accountability partner, to make sure you stay on track.

Most importantly, this is how you make your dreams a reality. This is how you make them into photos that become memories that you share with other people. This is how you get people excited and maybe jealous because your life has become uncommonly awesome. This is how the movie script you envisioned becomes a blockbuster of a life.

You've learned the importance of getting your desires out into the world. Writing them down or entering them on a computer is the first step. The capture list helps you get organized. Just get all those ideas out there. You don't have to make any commitment with the date behind them. Getting them out this way means that you won't forget them.

Before long the capture lists will become second nature to you. The language of action will be ingrained in you and will feel like it's always been there. You will have become one of the forty-one percent of people who no longer keep their dreams in their heads.

Then, when you move your items into your schedule, you're moving into action. You are now present in your own life. You start small, one bite at a time. One step at a time. One action each day. Now you are part of the five percent that are working toward living extraordinary lives.

How long is this going to take you? Realistically, about ten minutes a day is all you need to process your capture list. What's it costing you *not* to do this action? What's the gap in your life because you're not having that right now? I guarantee that it's more than ten minutes each day.

You've also learned that it's not just about scheduling items; it's choosing wisely how to spend your time. You're a person who lives a life of purpose, based on your priorities, not someone else's. You choose how to leverage your time and be in the cause and not living in the effect.

I grew up on a sailboat, which makes me a sucker for maritime analogies. When you put this plan into action, you realize that you're the captain of your ship. When you live in cause, you have the oar; you're harnessing the wind, and listening for where it's coming in. You can adjust the sails and stay true to your course of action.

Wouldn't you rather do that than to remain adrift in the hopes that someone else will come around and put the wind in your sails?

Remember, you can decide if you're going to embrace the highest levels of your divine masculine or feminine energy to create the life that matters, to create a life that's purposeful, meaningful, significant, and offers you inner peace and happiness.

Yes, moving from stress to success boils down to three little letters: Y-O-U.

TIME ISN'T THE PROBLEM TAKEAWAYS:

1. This is how I am adopting the methods in this book into my life.

CONCLUSION: ARE YOU READY TO TAKE ON THE WORLD?

What started me on this journey is the theory that we're all born equal. We're all given 168 hours in a week, twenty-four hours in a day. How we utilize that is what separates the boys from the men, or the amateurs from the professionals.

I looked at how some gurus and very talented people were able to build empires and be very fulfilled. I marveled at how somebody could run a multimillion company and still do some adventurous time-consuming thing like sailing or paragliding or even manage the simple pleasure of being at home for dinner with the kids and spouse. I came to see that it is about being decisive, deliberate, and very purposeful in your schedule.

But instead of saying it's all about work or it's all about just getting through life and surviving, these people put the value based things first in their schedule and then made room for everything else.

Too many people who don't accomplish as much tell themselves that they can't afford to live like that. Here's my challenge to that: What's the cost not to do that?

When you lead from your values and fill in with the other pieces, you're much more efficient and deliberate about not wasting a moment in those precious twenty-four hours.

WRITING YOUR OWN SCRIPT

On occasion, I will take time out of a normal session with my coaching clients and have them go through a dream experience or a visioning experience. There are many visioning methods out in the world today. The one I've embraced is from master coach, author, and visionary Peter Reding.

I'll have my clients close their eyes, and get their body into a very relaxed state. I will have a cloud come down, pick them up and carry them three years into the future. In a real session, this would take a certain amount of time, but the point is they are taken to who they are three years down the road in the future.

You can do this process for yourself. Find a quiet place to sit, put on some gentle, inspirational music, close your eyes, and breath slowly and rhythmically until you feel relaxed and at ease. As your body settles in, take a nice, deep breath and then exhale. Another deep breath and just let it go.

There's no right or wrong way to do this process. Anything that comes up for you or presents itself is absolutely perfect. You're totally safe, totally present. Take another deep breath and let yourself relax. Now imagine that there's a ball of warm, radiating light at the base of your feet. As you're lying there, this ball of light and energy is flowing into your feet sending relaxing waves of energy into your body.

The energy keeps moving through your feet to your heels, massaging, relaxing. Feel your feet relaxed. This ball of energy keeps moving into the ankles, up into the calves of your legs radiating warmth, relaxing waves of energy. The flowing of energy continues through the thighs, warm energy moving through the thighs into your torso. Just let your torso relax, let yourself relax.

The wave of energy flows into the back, the shoulders, the neck; massaging warm, relaxing waves of energy into the head, and the face. Feel this wave of relaxing energy flow into your arms and down into your fingers. Allow the energy to flow out through the tips of your fingers, leaving your body. Your body is now totally relaxed.

Now imagine yourself three years in the future. What does your life look like? Describe the surroundings in detail. It's your life; you're the only who has the power to dream this future. If you need help, use the movie analogy. What does the movie of your life look like three years from now? What do you want your future to look like? Take your time. Be specific. Stay with that image for as long as it takes to become crystal clear to you.

Then, when you're ready, you can sit up and open your eyes. Write it down in as much detail as possible. You will be glad you did.

Here's the good news. Now that you've read this book, you have the tools to start making that vision a reality!

Finally, I'll repeat something I've said several times in this book. Everything here is a guideline. It's not a law set in stone. If you read something that doesn't work for you, use only the parts that do.

The important point is that you take the action needed to live on your own terms, to be the hero of your own story. To live a life of purpose. A life that matters.

When you do this, a funny thing happens. You become the master of your time, and you will have transformed stress into success.

APPENDIX

Mind Maps

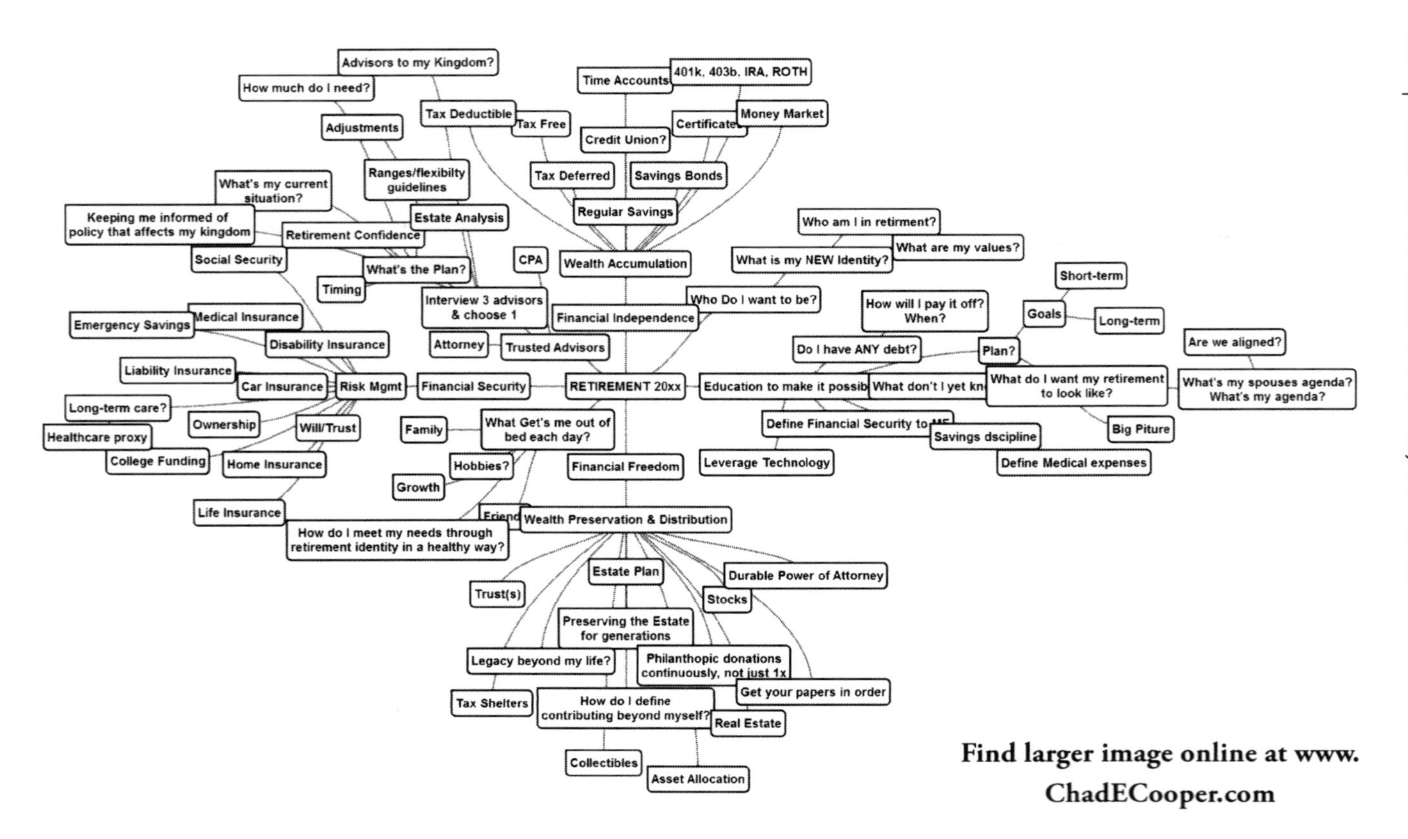

Find larger image online at www.ChadECooper.com

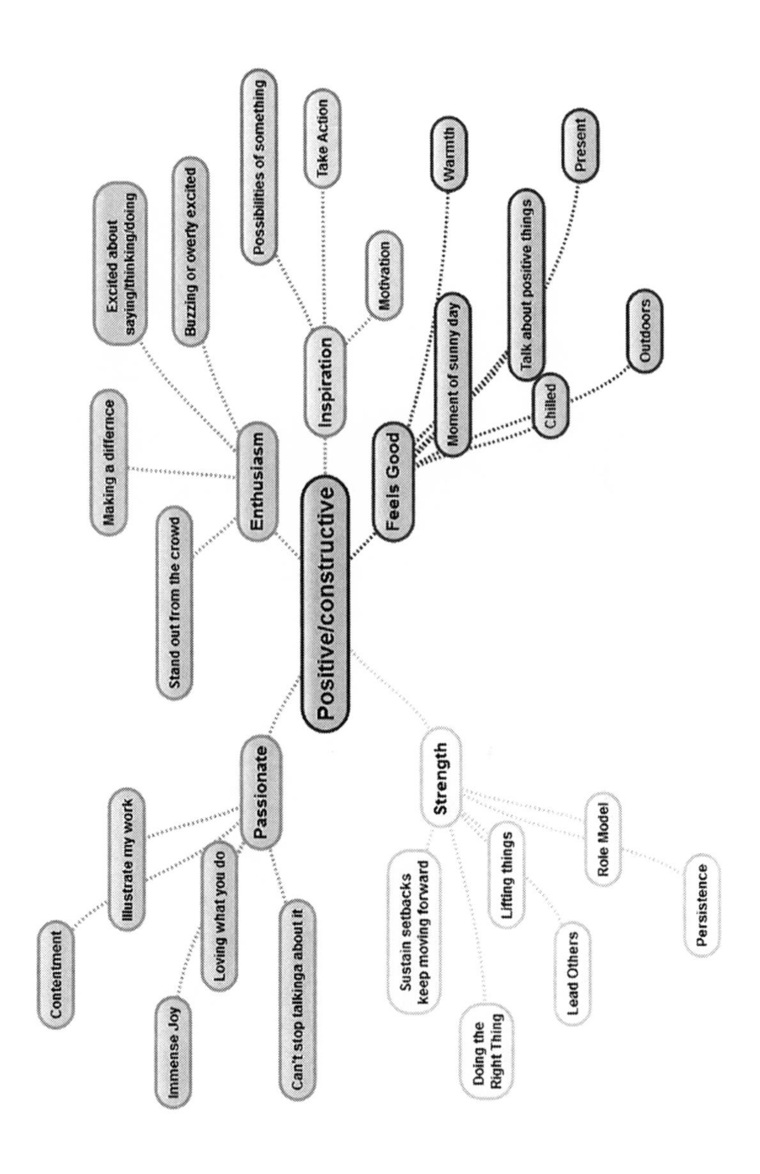

Find larger image online at www.ChadECooper.com

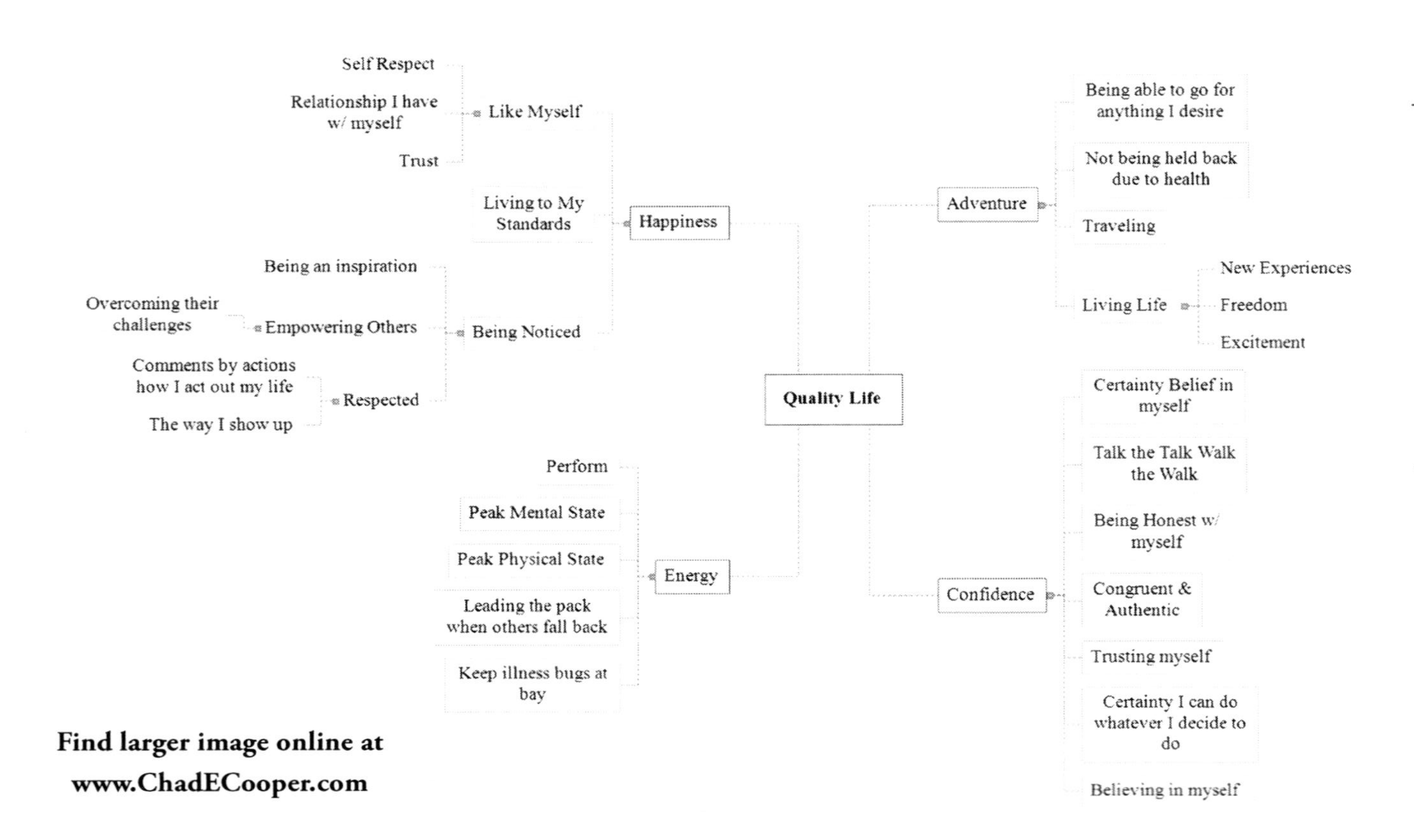
Self Respect
Relationship I have w/ myself
Trust
Like Myself
Living to My Standards
Happiness
Being an inspiration
Overcoming their challenges
Empowering Others
Being Noticed
Comments by actions how I act out my life
Respected
The way I show up
Quality Life
Perform
Peak Mental State
Peak Physical State
Energy
Leading the pack when others fall back
Keep illness bugs at bay
Adventure
Being able to go for anything I desire
Not being held back due to health
Traveling
Living Life
New Experiences
Freedom
Excitement
Confidence
Certainty Belief in myself
Talk the Talk Walk the Walk
Being Honest w/ myself
Congruent & Authentic
Trusting myself
Certainty I can do whatever I decide to do
Believing in myself
Find larger image online at
www.ChadECooper.com

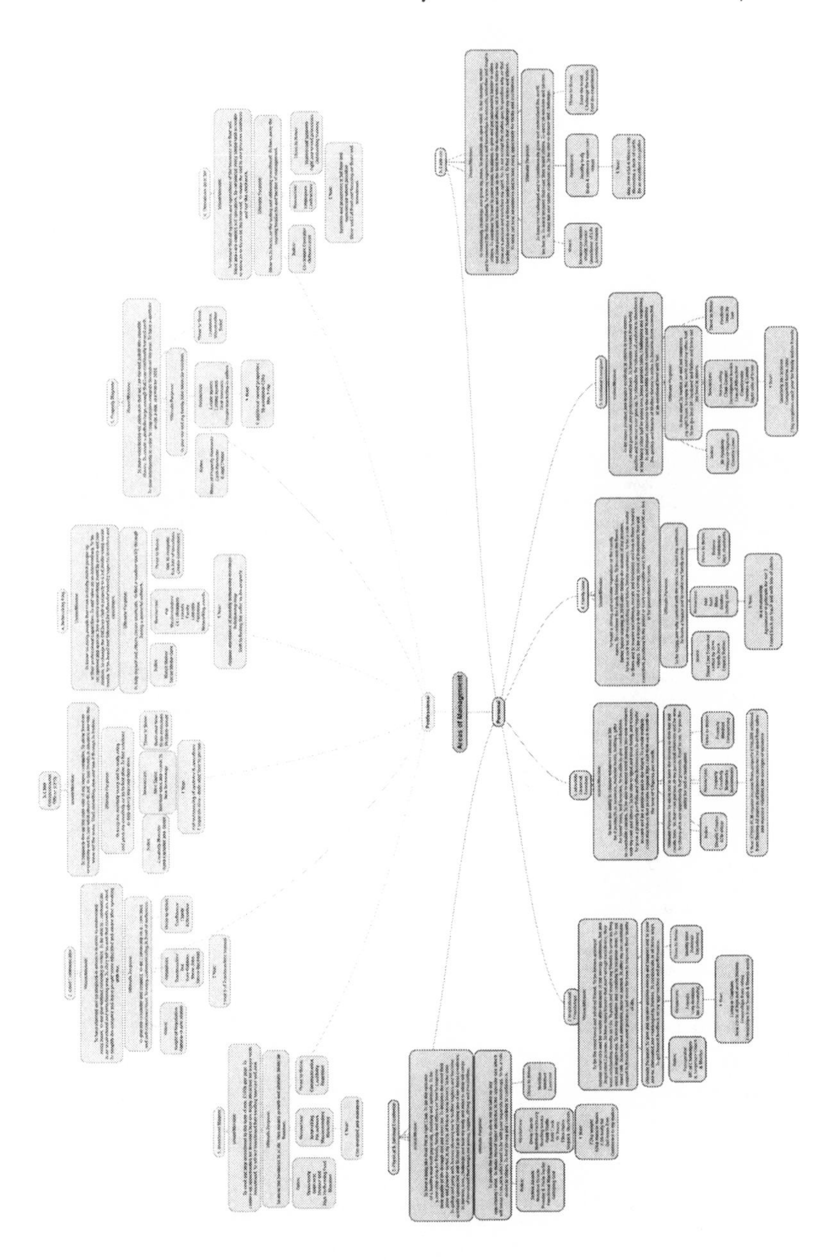

Find larger image online at www.ChadECooper.com

Chart showing movement of something from the three capture lists to the schedule (more can be found on www.ChadECooper.com)

- ☐ GB25 Heavenly's Gun Barrel event
- ☐ Swim w/ Manta Rays
- ☐ Land on and take off from an aircraft carrier
- ☐ Learn to snow ski
- ☐ Learn to waterski
- ☐ Read a book from each of the works of Shakespeare, Plato, Aristotle, Dickens, Thoreau, Rousseau,
- ☐ Play Clair de Lune on the piano
- ☐ Visit a movie studio
- ☐ Solve a Rubik's Cube
- ☐ Complete the Norseman Extreme Triathlon
- ☐ Play the Old Course at St. Andrews
- ☐ Fly in a Hot Air Balloon Over the Loire Valley*
- ☐ Swim With Manatees
- ☐ Mackinac Island Michigan
- ☐ Complete a Big Game Adventure
- ☐ Eat a Crocodile Meat
- ☐ Dye my Clothes
- ☐ Dye my Hair Purple
- ☐ Drive More Than , Km in One Year
- ☐ Drink a $ Bottle of Wine
- ☐ Drink Different Cocktails
- ☐ Dress a Man
- ☐ Draw Funny Faces on all the Eggs in my Fridge
- ☐ Don't Use the Phone For a Day
- ☐ Don't Talk a Whole Day
- ☐ Do Something Unexpected
- ☐ Do Something Absolutely Spontaneous
- ☐ Do Everything With my Left Hand For a Whole Day
- ☐ Do a Strip Tease on a Pole
- ☐ Do a New Year Dip
- ☐ Discover the Lost City of Atlantis
- ☐ Dine in the Eiffel Tower
- ☐ Dine at Sanyou Cave Hanging Cliff Restaurant, China
- ☐ Dance all Around the World
- ☐ Cross Abbey Road Crosswalk in London
- ☐ Create a World Map With Pins of Where I've Been
- ☐ Crash a Party
- ☐ Cover a Car in Post-It's
- ☐ Complete the IMDB Top Movies
- ☐ Color my Hair Blue
- ☐ Collect Sand from Countries
- ☐ Collect Autographs from all my Favorite People
- ☐ Collect a Penny For Every Year I've Lived
- ☐ Collect a Jar of Dirt from Every State
- ☐ Collect a Coin from Every Country I Visit
- ☐ Collect Shotglasses
- ☐ Climb a Light House
- ☐ Climb a Coconut Tree Barefoot
- ☐ Chew Khat
- ☐ Change my Name
- ☐ Change Clothing in a Phone box
- ☐ Celebrate my Birthday in Another Country
- ☐ Cartwheel Along the Golden Gate Bridge
- ☐ Camel Race in the Desert
- ☐ Call Someone, Tell Them to Look Out Their Window, and Be Standing on Their Front Lawn
- ☐ Buy Someone's Groceries Just Because
- ☐ Bum Around America in a Van
- ☐ Box a Kangaroo
- ☐ Book a Dive to the Titanic
- ☐ Book a Commercial Flight to Space
- ☐ Blow Bubbles in the Rain
- ☐ Black Taxi Ride in London

WHEEL OF LIFE

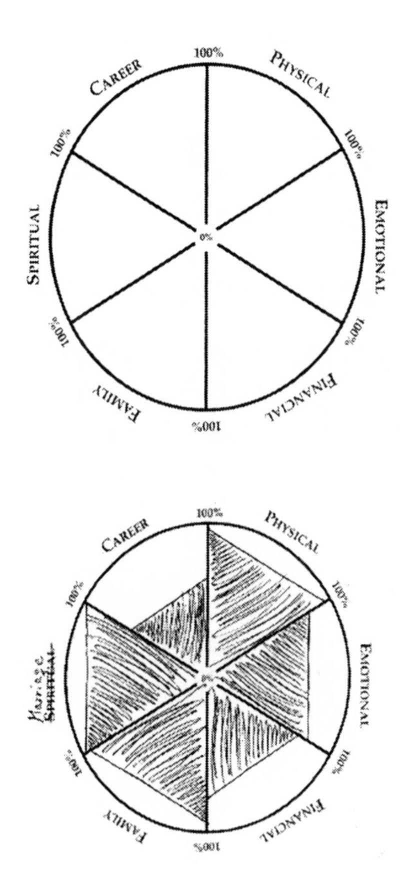

Find larger image online at www.ChadECooper.com

SURVEY RESULTS

1. Are you currently retired?

Value	Count	Percent
No	600	100.0%
Yes	0	0.0%

2. Do you live in the state of California?

Value	Count	Percent
No	0	0.0%
Yes	600	100.0%

3. How old are you?

Value	Count	Percent
Under 50	0	0.0%
50-57	373	62.2%
58-65	227	37.8%
Over 65	0	0.0%

Statistics	
Total Responses	600
Sum	31,816.0
Avg.	53
StdDev	3.9
Max	58

4. Thinking about your life overall, how would you say you've done so far in achieving your goals, on a scale of 1-10 where "1" is "Not at all well" and "10" is "I've achieved virtually every goal I've set?"

Value		Count	Percent		
1 - Not at all well		6	1.0%		
	2	6	1.0%		
	3	13	2.2%		
	4	27	4.5%		
	5	47	7.8%		
	6	94	15.7%		
	7	167	27.8%		
	8	173	28.8%	8+	40.0%
	9	55	9.2%	7+	67.8%
10 - You've achieved virtually every goal I've set?		12	2.0%		

Sum	
Avg.	6.9
StdDev	1.6
Max	10

Find larger image online at www.ChadECooper.com

5. Looking at the following list, what are the TOP 3 things you'd like to spend more time with or more time doing?

Value	Count	Percent	
Your children	202	33.7%	5
Your spouse or partner	289	48.2%	2
Contributing to your community	131	21.8%	
Working	68	11.3%	
Pursuing your hobbies	237	39.5%	4
In spiritual practice	81	13.5%	
Managing your finances	62	10.3%	
Taking vacation	347	57.8%	1
Personal development (fitness, nutrition, meditation, etc.)	267	44.5%	3
Celebration	32	5.3%	
Other (please specify)	33	5.5%	

6. We'd like to know a little about how you set goals. Please tell us how well each of the following describes your goal-setting, where "1" is "doesn't describe you at all" and "5" is "describes you perfectly"

	1—Not at		2		3		4		5—Perfec		Response		
	%	#	%	#	%	#	%	#	%	#	#		
When you set a goal, you always make sure it's actions	2.3%	14	7.0%	42	26.3%	158	49.5%	297	14.8%	89	600	9.3%	
You don't set goals more than 6 months in advance	23.0%	138	23.7%	142	28.7%	172	18.7%	112	6.0%	36	600	28.0%	
You always write your goals down	35.7%	214	24.8%	149	19.7%	118	13.3%	80	6.5%	39	600	60.5%	2
You have written life goals	46.9%	281	19.7%	118	14.7%	88	11.8%	71	5.3%	32	600	66.2%	1
You make your goals as specific as possible	7.8%	47	19.8%	119	31.8%	191	28.3%	170	12.2%	73	600	27.6%	5
You have written down what you want to do or accompl	46.3%	278	18.5%	111	16.7%	100	12.0%	72	6.5%	39	600	64.8%	3
You make sure your goals have measurable outcomes	9.7%	58	17.7%	106	27.0%	162	33.3%	200	12.2%	73	600	27.4%	
You always set a deadline or date by which you want to	18.2%	109	26.0%	156	31.7%	190	19.3%	116	4.8%	29	600	44.2%	4
You strive to make your goals realistic	2.3%	14	6.5%	39	22.7%	136	47.0%	282	22.2%	133	600	8.9%	

7. When you think about retirement, how do you feel about it on a scale of 1-10, where "1" is "you dread even thinking about retirement" and "10" is "you can't wait to retire?"

Value	Count	Percent		
1—You dread even thinking about it	16	2.7%		
2	19	3.2%		
3	27	4.5%		
4	22	3.7%		
5	54	9.0%		
6	64	10.7%		
7	100	16.7%		
8	109	18.2%	8+	49.7%
9	76	12.7%	7+	65.8%
10—You can't wait to retire	113	18.8%		

Find larger image online at www.ChadECooper.com

8. Do you have a unique ability, skill, or passion that you haven't been able to pursue that you want to be able to pursue in retirement?

Value	Count	Percent
No	313	52.2%
Yes	287	47.8%

10. For which of the following do you have concrete, written goals? Please choose all that apply.

Value	Count	Percent
How you will prepare for retirement	284	47.4%
What you will do in retirement	227	37.9%
When you will retire	227	37.9%

11. How much of the time would you say you experience or do each of the following:

	Almost al		Most of th		Some of tl		Almost ne		Response		
	%	#	%	#	%	#	%	#	#		
You feel overwhelmed	2.7%	16	10.8%	65	56.8%	341	29.7%	178	600	13.5%	
You dare to dream	20.7%	124	33.5%	201	39.0%	234	6.8%	41	600	45.8%	5
You spend a lot of time contributing to others	12.0%	72	38.8%	233	43.5%	261	5.7%	34	600	49.2%	3
You check your email almost constantly during the day	32.2%	193	31.8%	191	27.3%	164	8.7%	52	600	64.0%	1
You set limits on yourself	5.2%	31	36.0%	216	48.3%	290	10.5%	63	600	41.2%	
You feel it's possible to design your own life	17.0%	102	44.0%	264	32.0%	192	7.0%	42	600	39.0%	
You feel you're doing exactly what you want to do	9.8%	59	42.3%	254	40.7%	244	7.2%	43	600	47.8%	4
You believe in your own potential	33.5%	201	45.3%	272	18.3%	110	2.8%	17	600	21.1%	
You feel your life is out of balance	5.5%	33	16.3%	98	47.0%	282	31.2%	187	600	21.8%	
You spend a lot of time doing things that feel good but	2.0%	12	13.2%	79	52.7%	316	32.2%	193	600	15.2%	
You keep most of your "to dos" in your head, rather tha	23.7%	142	34.7%	208	26.8%	161	14.8%	89	600	58.4%	2
You don't have enough discretion in your life	2.8%	17	16.0%	96	46.0%	276	35.2%	211	600	18.8%	
You focus on "to dos," rather than outcomes	6.3%	38	33.2%	199	48.0%	288	12.5%	75	600	39.5%	
You plan your day carefully, as opposed to "letting it un	8.2%	49	37.3%	224	44.7%	268	9.8%	59	600	54.8%	6

12. Which of the following do you use to schedule or plan? Please choose all that apply.

Value	Count	Percent	
A smartphone	246	41.0%	4
A paper calendar	282	47.0%	3
A computer or online calendar	321	53.5%	1
A "to do" or task list (whether paper or digital)	301	50.2%	2
"Post it" notes	220	36.7%	5
A day planner	112	18.7%	
Mind mapping	99	16.5%	
Other (please specify)	20	3.3%	

Find larger image online at www.ChadECooper.com

13. How old are you?

Value	Count	Percent
Under 18	0	0.0%
18-24	1	0.2%
25-34	0	0.0%
Under 50	2	0.3%
50-60	457	76.2%
60-65	138	23.0%
65-74	2	0.3%
75 or above	0	0.0%

14. What is the highest level of school or college that you've completed?

Value	Count	Percent
Some high school	1	0.2%
High school degree	32	5.3%
Some college	166	27.7%
College degree	176	29.3%
Some graduate work	50	8.3%
Graduate degree (MA/MS, PhD, JD, etc.)	175	29.2%

15. Are you . . .

Value	Count	Percent
Male	300	50.0%
Female	300	50.0%

16. Do you . . .

Value	Count	Percent
Own your own business	113	18.8%
Work for someone else	369	61.5%
Both	73	12.2%
Neither	45	7.5%

Find larger image online at www.ChadECooper.com

WORKBOOK PAGES

Please refer to www.ChadECooper.com and go to section for workbook action. Under this section is an online tool to assist in where you currently spend your week (aka168 hours) and strategies on how to increase getting more out of that same amount of time.

Sample Schedules: www.ChadECooper.com

BIBLIOGRAPHY

Chapman, Gary. *The 5 Love Languages: The Secret to Love That Lasts.* Northfield Publishing, 2010.

Covey, Steven. *The 7 Habits of Highly Effective People: Powerful Lessons in Personal Change.* New York, Simon & Schuster, 1990.

Frankl, Viktor, *Man's Search for Meaning.* Boston, Beacon, 2006.

Hendrickson, Pam and Koenigs, Mike, *Make, Market, Launch IT: The Ultimate Product Creation System for Turning Your Ideas Into Income.* Product Solutions Group, LLC, 2013.

Hill, Napoleon. *Think and Grow Rich.* New York, Tarcher. Revised Ed. 2005. Originally published in 1937.

Katz, Elliot. *Being the Strong Man a Woman Wants: Timeless Wisdom on Being a Man.* Award Press. 2005.

Klinenberg, Eric. *Going Solo: The Extraordinary Rise and Surprising Appeal of Living Alone.* Center Point Press, 2012.

Ruiz, don Miguel. *The Four Agreements: A Practical Guide to Personal Freedom, A Toltec Wisdom Book.* Amber-Allen Publishing, 2001.

Stets, Jan E. and Burke, Peter J. *Femininity/Masculinity*. Department of Sociology, Washington State University. Borgatta, Edward F. and Montgomery, Rhonda J.V. (eds.). *Encyclopedia of Sociology, Revised Edition*. New York, Macmillan. (p. 997-1005)

Tolle, Eckhart. *A New Earth: Awakening to Your Life's Purpose*. New York. Penguin. 2008.

Pp. 997-1005 in Edgar F. Borgatta and Rhonda J. V. Montgomery (Eds.), Encyclopedia of Sociology, Revised Edition. New York: Macmillan.

If we live by society's standards – it's a pretty low bar – we're going to end up having some problems. When you live by your standards and you implement them; your relationship with your spouse, your children, and your boss will improve. But most importantly your relationship with yourself will enable you to live a life that matters.

—Chad E. Cooper